Let's go time traveling!

Through the magic of history, we'll relive the events that created the place we call home. We'll return to the days of the fur trappers, the riverboat captains, the cowpunchers and the railroad workers — all the men and women, boys and girls who built Kansas City and the area around it.

In this book, each chapter begins with Time Traveler, who will set the scene for you. Then, the stories begin. Some of the most interesting and important people, places and events are marked in **boldface type**. In back, there's a glossary to help you with words that may be unfamiliar.

Journeys Through Time

A YOUNG TRAVELER'S GUIDE TO KANSAS CITY'S HISTORY

Monroe Dodd   Daniel Serda

A KC150 Project

Funding provided by the William T. Kemper Foundation, Commerce Bank, Trustee, and the Kansas City Star Co.

Kansas City Star Books

Journeys Through Time

A YOUNG TRAVELER'S GUIDE
TO KANSAS CITY'S HISTORY

Information based on Kansas City: An American Story *by Rick Montgomery and Shirl Kasper, edited by Monroe Dodd.* **Copyright © 1999 the Kansas City Star Co.**

Book Design
Jean Donaldson Dodd

Associate Editor
Les Weatherford

Graphics
Dave Eames

Consultants
Dana Bart, Cassandra Lopez, Jennifer Roe, Penny Selle

Cover photos:
Front cover, top row from left: Harry S. Truman with Thomas J. Pendergast; the Battle of Westport by N.C. Wyeth; an Osage mother and her child; a fur trapper. Second row: Opening day at Union Station, 1914; Bennie Moten and his orchestra at Fairyland Park, 1931. Bottom row; children at the City Union Mission, about 1930; the town of Kansas, early 1850s. Back cover, top: "Sky Stations" at Bartle Hall, early 1990s; second row, Metcalf South Shopping Center, 1960s; Ewing Kauffman; the Country Club Plaza; bottom row, the Junction — Ninth, Main and Delaware streets, 1906.

Introduction photos:
   i: About 1930, these three children had an outdoor tea party with their dog as a guest.
   ii-iii: Turn-of-the-century children and adults posed on a pleasant day.
   iv-v: In 1881 men, women and children stood on flooded streets at a grocery on Ninth Street in the West Bottoms.
   vi: Left: Children, adult, horse and dog in the late 1800s. Center: Dressed in their finest clothes, these unidentified children and women sat for a group photo in the 1910s. Right: A birthday party in the 1920s.
   vii: Two girls outside the Street Hotel, 18th and the Paseo, in the late 1940s or early 1950s.

Published by KANSAS CITY STAR BOOKS
1729 Grand Boulevard, Kansas City, Missouri 64108

First Edition

Library of Congress Card Number: 00-103530

ISBN 0-9679519-0-9

Printed in the United States of America
by Walsworth Publishing Co.

Table of Contents

Time traveling

Have you ever wondered what it would be like to live in the past? What it was like to live in a world without electricity, television, or telephones?

This book and the stories in it are designed to do just that — to transport you to the past, as if you were in a time machine. Using words, pictures, maps, and activities, this book will take you — along with your friends and your imagination — into the history of this place we call Kansas City. You will understand how the place we live affects the patterns of our daily lives.

Sometimes, history can seem a chore — or even a bore. The writers of this book have tried hard to keep from drowning you in details. We won't be quizzing you about dates, although we will talk about important events. We don't expect you to remember the name of every person we discuss. However, we think you *will* remember a lot of what you read. We hope you'll even want to learn more about the exciting and challenging twists and turns encountered by all the people who lived before us.

Each chapter of this book presents the story of an era, or period of time, in our past. Along the way, you will learn the stories that make our city a unique and important place to all of our lives.

And you will discover how to time travel on your own.

The word "his*tory*" hints at one way to time travel — through stories about the past. These can be stories about boys and girls like you, stories about great accomplishments, sometimes huge failures, impressive achievements, and even frightening disasters.

Remember, though, that these stories were not made up — or meant to entertain. They are real stories about real things. And often that can be more entertaining than made-up stories!

Digging up information about the past can be fun, too. Understanding the past requires research, or detective work, that can be exciting. It can lead us to great discoveries and insights.

That's history — the practice of learning about the past through written records, through books, through artifacts, through stories passed down from grandparent to grandchild. When you finish this book, you'll not only know a lot more about Kansas City, but you'll also be equipped to venture out on your own. You can be a historian, too.

Our voyage begins where you are sitting now — only we'll start more than two hundred years in the past. Before we leave on our voyage, the captain has asked that you clear your mind. Forget about television, about automobiles, about VCRs, CD players, video games, even electricity. Use your imagination to travel to a time when there were no highways, no streets, no sidewalks, no television and no Internet. Then, all of Kansas City was vast, open land and forest, and only the footprints of our ancestors marked the paths followed every day by boys and girls just like you.

Now our journey can begin.

CHAPTER ONE

Earliest times ~ 1853

Bend of the river

Great forces of nature shaped the place where we live.

Two hundred million years ago, scientists say, a vast ocean covered all of what is now Kansas City. When the ocean disappeared, it left behind thick layers of sediment that became what we call limestone. You can see traces of this sea — including the fossilized remains of trilobites and other ancient creatures — everywhere. These traces range from the yellowish outcroppings along roads and highways to pebbles in your back yard.

About 18,000 years ago, large sheets of ice called glaciers stretched south from Canada into the area where the Kansas River would join the Missouri. The glaciers carved bluffs and set the course of the Missouri River.

Various people have been enchanted by the idea of our landscape as a place of natural beauty and untapped riches. The Spanish explorer Coronado ventured into central Kansas in 1541. He was seeking Quivira, a land that ancient myths claimed was built entirely of gold.

Now, more than 250 years later, we have traveled through time to the early 1800s. President Thomas Jefferson has overseen the Louisiana Purchase. The acquisition claims much of the Midwest from the French. This vast territory, Jefferson believes, will help create the ideal American who will earn a living for his family by working the earth.

West of the original 13 colonies, great forests and lush river valleys stretch toward this area. Near the Kansas River's junction with the Missouri, there is a sharp change from these forests. West of the region lie vast and open plains, rolling land with few trees,

TIME TRAVELER

stretching as far as the eye can see.

In the early 1820s a report of a government expedition led by Maj. Stephen Long declares much of this land "unfit for human habitation." Soon newspapers and national magazines begin to refer to this new frontier as the "Great American Desert."

When it creates the new state of Missouri, the federal government establishes a boundary between the forests and the plains at the same spot the glaciers did. Everything West is called the "badlands." As Native Americans are forced out of states like Ohio and Indiana, they will be resettled into this land. It is officially renamed Indian Territory.

As you can imagine, early settlers will not take kindly to their part of the world being referred to as a desert. So they set out to create an opposite impression. The West, they proclaim, is actually a garden spot, a beautiful slice of nature that is a perfect fit not only for Jefferson's yeoman farmers, but also for a landscape that will soon give rise to some of the grandest cities ever seen.

At the boundary between Missouri and Indian Territory, a new settlement soon arises. The locals call it "Kansas," after the river and the Indian tribe that gave the river its name.

Geographers use the word "landscape" not only to describe nature, but also to tell how people change the land and understand their place in the environment. Kansas City's ideas about its landscape will always be on the boundary, between civilization and frontier; between two states; between country and city. As we will discover, these contrasts — and our feelings about the natural and manmade landscape — will shape our understanding of our city, our region and ourselves.

This was a crossroads. Just imagine...

In downtown Kansas City you can stand on the old river bluffs and let your imagination soar.

A park at Eighth and Jefferson streets overlooks the Missouri River. Below, airplanes buzz into and out of the airport. Freight trains curl into the West Bottoms. Trucks and cars whiz by on interstate highways.

This place has always been a crossroads. It was a crossroads even before there were airports and railroads and interstate highways.

Confluence of the Missouri and Kansas rivers.

Now use your imagination. Imagine a time when the Missouri River was the nation's superhighway — first for Indian canoes and then for the boats of European settlers. Imagine these craft landing. First came the Indians. Later came French-speaking fur traders. Then English-speaking farmers and business owners. And then the river brought traders and pioneers setting out on the Santa Fe, the Oregon and the California trails.

Here, Missouri River travelers began heading north, or left the river to travel west or southwest. Some even floated up the Kansas River. Early settlers called this area Kawsmouth, using the Kansas River's informal name, the Kaw.

So nature created the first roads in this river valley. Then human beings created their own roads. By 1821 this area was home to a permanent settlement. By the 1830s it was beginning to see more and more traffic in boats and wagons. In the 1850s it became a city — Kansas City.

This is how it was born.

French-speaking fur trappers loved a party. The drawing of this dance around the campfire was made by Alfred Jacob Miller.

Trappers ranged far into the plains and mountains to get furs. Beaver pelts were used to make hats. Left: This trapper, painted by Alfred Jacob Miller, was named Louis.

Forests and plains

The Kansas City region lies in what geologists call the Central Lowlands, which cover much of the Midwest. Our area lies at the southernmost point that the glaciers reached about 18,000 years ago. In the mid-19th century the Kansas City area stood at the western edge of the vast eastern forests. Just to the west, treeless prairies and plains took over. Can you imagine what your neighborhood looked like then?

Early Residents

Native Americans

Beginning about 500 B.C. various Indian cultures came and went in the region that today is Missouri and Kansas.

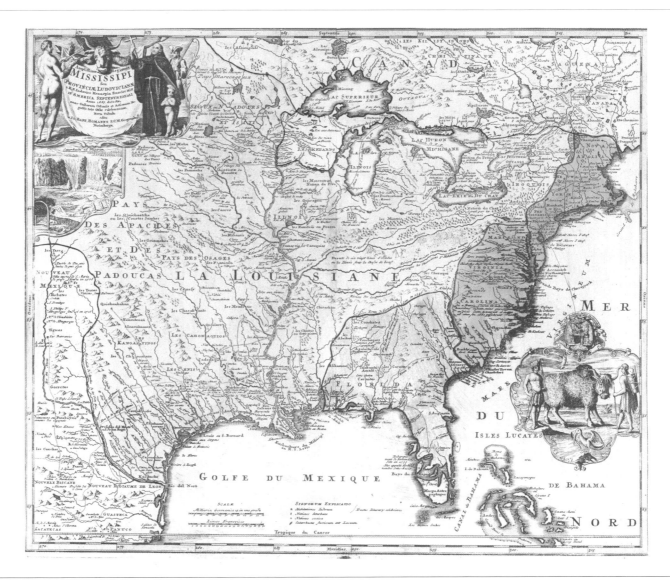

Then, around 1500 or 1600 A.D., the **Missouri** people arrived. The Missouri lived mostly north of the river that now bears their name. Not long after the Missouri arrived, two tribes, the **Kansa** and the **Osage**, left their lands in the East and came to our area. The Osage built villages mostly south of the Missouri River in today's Missouri.

The Kansa inhabited lands that today are northeast Kansas and northwest Missouri.

By the time the 1700s ended, the Kansa lived mostly west of Kawsmouth, up the Kansas River. The Osage dominated lands east of that. The Missouri, diminished in numbers, had been forced out by other Indian cultures.

An Osage mother and her child

A Kansa chief, White Plume

European claims

In 1682, French explorers claimed the Mississippi River basin for King Louis XIV. What is now Missouri and most of Kansas lay in this vast area, named **Louisiana** after the king. Through the 1700s the only Europeans in the area of Kawsmouth were explorers and trappers who passed through. The nearest city established by Europeans was **St. Louis**, which was built by French-speakers as a trading center in 1764. The same year, they learned that France had transferred the entire territory of Louisiana to Spain. In spite of Spanish rule, most residents continued to speak French. In the early 1800s, Louisiana territory returned briefly to France.

This map of the Louisiana territory was made in 1759. It is marked in Latin and French.

Becoming America

In 1803 the United States bought the Louisiana Territory from France.
This was called the Louisiana Purchase.

This land, much of which the French had not even explored, vastly increased the size of the United States. To find out what it was like, President Thomas Jefferson sent **Meriwether Lewis** and **William Clark** on an expedition of discovery. Lewis and Clark left St. Louis and headed up the Missouri River. On June 26, 1804, their boats passed the site of today's Kansas City. They camped on the "upper point of the mouth of the river Kanzas." They passed again on their return home in 1806.

The Lewis and Clark expedition is memorialized by this statue overlooking Kawsmouth.

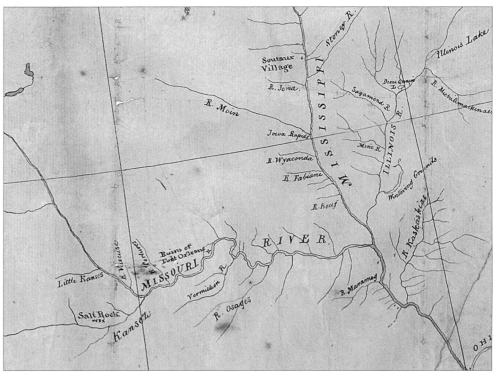

A map used by the explorers. Meriwether Lewis made notes on it.

Fort Osage was reconstructed on its original site and can be visited today. The fort and the Osage boundary are shown on the 1820 map at right. Note how no towns existed in the area at that time.

The Osage treaty

Hoping to ensure good relations between American settlers and the Osage, the United States in 1808 established **Fort Osage**. The fort was not so much for military activity as for trading goods with the Osage. The fort was situated several miles downriver from Kawsmouth. The Osage, meanwhile, wanted the protection of the U.S. government. So they agreed to a treaty giving up 200 square miles of their land between the Missouri and the Arkansas rivers. The western boundary of this land would be a north-south line through Fort

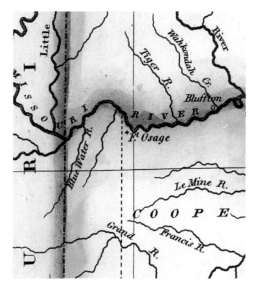

Osage. That line was about six miles east of today's Missouri-Kansas border.

A new state

In 1812, Congress created the **Territory of Missouri** out of the Louisiana Purchase. This was aimed at meeting demands of settlers for a better government organization.

Among other things, this organization was expected to handle land claims more easily. Yet by 1818 many Missourians were convinced that they deserved more — full equality with other Americans in the form of statehood.

In 1821 the **state of Missouri** was admitted into the union. This gave Americans in Missouri their own government, including offices to buy and sell property and settle disputes.

It also introduced a new slave state into the United States. Missouri's entry as a state that allowed slavery was balanced by the entry of Maine as a free state.

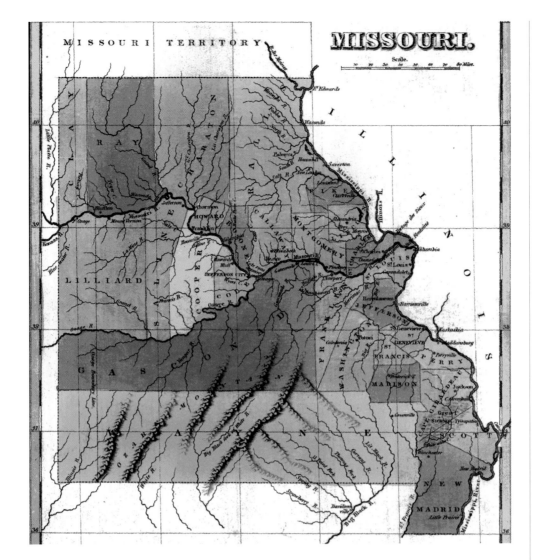

Missouri in the 1820s.

First European settlers

Francois Chouteau and his wife, **Berenice Chouteau**, led a group of settlers up the Missouri River in 1821 to establish a trading post. They set it up a few miles down the river from Kawsmouth.

Chouteau, who spoke French, was a representative of the wealthy Chouteau family of St. Louis, which handled much of the fur trade of the west. Beaver and other animals were killed by far-ranging hunters and trappers. The animals' furry coats were shipped east to be made into hats and other clothing. Francois Chouteau's operation was the first European settlement in the area, and some historians have called Chouteau the founder of Kansas City.

There is no sign that Francois Chouteau ever expected his outpost and its homes and farms to become a city. Nevertheless a French-speaking community grew up around Chouteau's business. It contained fur trappers and their wives, who in many cases were Indian women.

Other neighbors, with French names such as Prudhomme, were farmers. By the late 1820s, English-sounding names were beginning to outnumber French-sounding names in the area.

The powerful Chouteau family of St. Louis was led by Jean Pierre, left, and Auguste, right.

Getting organized

In 1822 English-speaking settlers formed **Clay County** on the north side of the Missouri River and established **Liberty** as its county seat.

In 1825 the Osage made a treaty with the United States giving up their rights to the western edge of Missouri. They moved to a reservation in what would become southern Kansas. English-speaking settlers began moving in to their former land south of the Missouri River.

In 1826, **Jackson County** was organized. In 1827, **Independence** was chosen to be the county seat. In 1828 a land office opened to handle buying and selling of land.

The Platte Purchase

Originally, Missouri's northwest boundary did not extend to the Missouri River. The state line ran north and south from the mouth of the Kansas River, where it emptied into the Missouri. In the 1830s, Missourians wanted to farm the rich land just west of the state line and east of the Missouri River. They asked Congress to annex, or add, the area to the state of Missouri.

Congress agreed, and in 1837 Missouri grew by about 2 million acres. The Iowa and the Sac and Fox Indians, who had been moved there only a few years earlier, had to move again.

This land was called the **Platte**

Purchase, after a river that ran through it. The southern part of this was organized in 1839 into **Platte County**. The county seat was **Platte City**.

Early Settlement

1820s and 1830s
This is how our area may have looked in the time of Chouteau's trading post.

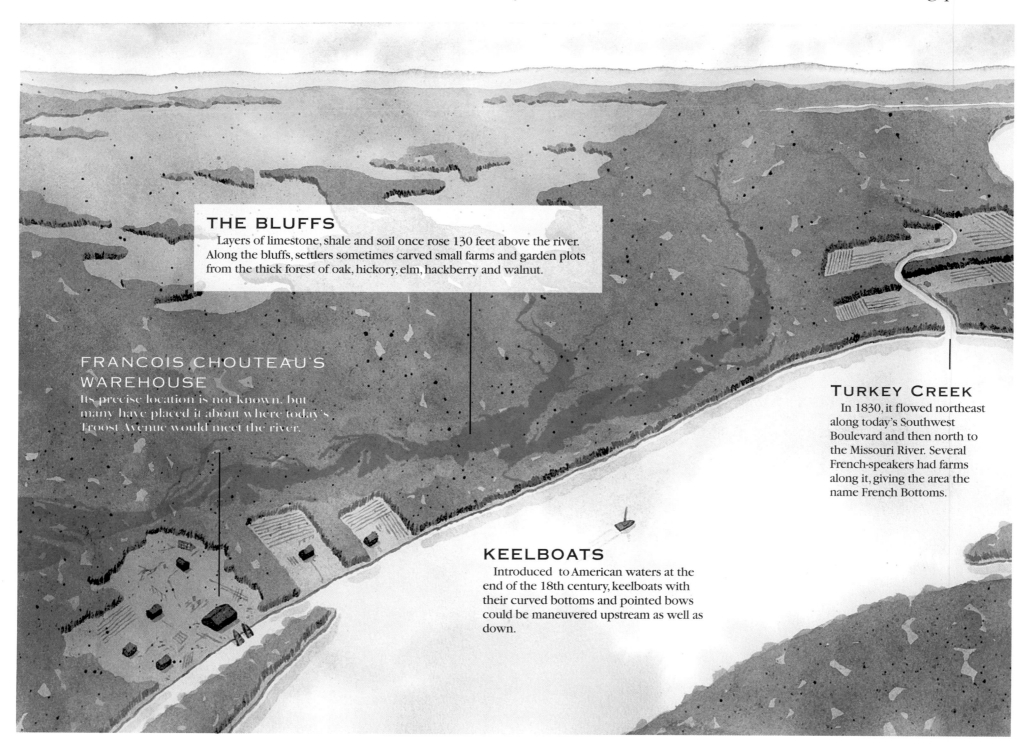

THE BLUFFS
Layers of limestone, shale and soil once rose 130 feet above the river. Along the bluffs, settlers sometimes carved small farms and garden plots from the thick forest of oak, hickory, elm, hackberry and walnut.

FRANCOIS CHOUTEAU'S WAREHOUSE
Its precise location is not known, but many have placed it about where today's Troost Avenue would meet the river.

TURKEY CREEK
In 1830, it flowed northeast along today's Southwest Boulevard and then north to the Missouri River. Several French-speakers had farms along it, giving the area the name French Bottoms.

KEELBOATS
Introduced to American waters at the end of the 18th century, keelboats with their curved bottoms and pointed bows could be maneuvered upstream as well as down.

This is an artist's conception, based on descriptions from that era and from later written memories and photographs. This view looks southwest. On the south bank of the river — where downtown Kansas City would rise one day — there were bluffs, ridges and ravines. Climbing them and heading south from the river, the forests eventually gave way to rolling prairies.

On the River

Long ago, the Missouri River was filled with snags and sandbars. This painting by Swiss artist Karl Bodmer shows how the river looked in 1833 a few miles downstream from Fort Osage.

Rivers were the superhighways of the American frontier. On rivers, boats did what cars and trucks do on today's highways.

French trappers traveled on narrow boats called **pirogues**. These were hollowed-out logs propelled by paddles or poles.

Big loads of furs or other materials were shipped downstream on **flatboats**. These were simple, cheap and easily built craft shaped much like the river barges of today. **Keelboats** could travel well upstream or down. They had a long shape, a narrow bow and stern, and a curved bottom. Although keelboats could fly sails, their power to go upstream usually came from a six- to 10-man crew. Crew members used long poles to push off the bottom and sometimes swam ashore to pull the boat with long tow ropes.

The first **steamboat** trip on the Missouri River occurred in 1819. That year the Independence, designed especially for the shallow waters of the Missouri, took 13 days to go from St. Louis to Franklin, which was near today's Boonville.

Flatboat

Keelboat

Steamboat

The Church

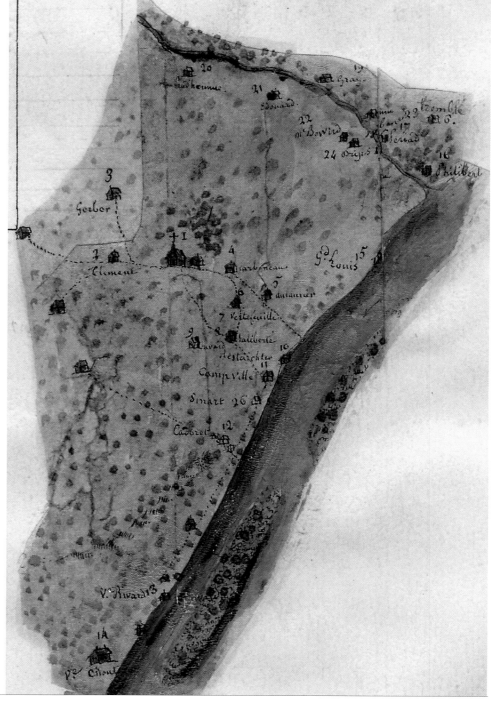

The first church in the Chouteau settlement along the Missouri, **St. Francis Regis**, was opened in 1834. Chouteau family money paid for it, and the priest was **Father Benedict Roux**. His native language was French. Before long, however, he had to use his English; Americans were moving in.

Nicolas Point was a Jesuit missionary who spent a few months preaching at St. Francis Regis in 1840 and 1841. He drew these illustrations while he was here. The sketch above depicted wagons heading south past the tiny church. His bird's-eye view at right showed the church at No. 1 and the homes of local Catholic families. The view looks southwest across the Missouri River. At top is Turkey Creek, which then entered the Missouri. Today its course takes it into the Kansas River.

The Mormons

Mormons being tarred and feathered.

The **Church of Jesus Christ of Latter-day Saints** was founded as a small group in 1830 in New York. Its members were known as Saints or as **Mormons** (after the Book of Mormon, a text revealed to their founder). They were often persecuted and moved from place to place.

In 1831 some moved to Jackson County, Mo. In Independence, the founder of the church had predicted, Mormons could find safety when Judgment Day arrived. But previous settlers distrusted the Mormons. The Mormons did not believe in slavery and called themselves the chosen people.

After an anti-slavery editorial was published in the Mormon newspaper, non-Mormon settlers destroyed the paper's press. They also drove several Mormons from their homes. That led the group to move across the Missouri River to Clay County and later to northwest Missouri.

In 1838, Gov. Lilburn W. Boggs ordered the Mormons "exterminated or driven from the state." Fifteen thousand Missouri Mormons left that winter for Illinois.

After their leader, **Joseph Smith**, was killed in 1844, dissension arose. Some members followed **Brigham Young** to Utah. Others stayed behind in Illinois, and in 1860 one group established the **Reorganized Church of Jesus Christ of Latter Day Saints**. This group eventually moved back to Missouri. Today the RLDS headquarters is in Independence, and many members live in the Kansas City area.

Indian Territory

The land just west of Missouri was where the U.S. government was moving tribes that had been in the path of white settlement in eastern states.

One of these tribes was the **Delaware**, whose home had been the Atlantic coast and later Missouri. In 1829 the Delaware were assigned to what today is called Wyandotte and Leavenworth counties with more land to the west.

The **Shawnee** in 1825 were assigned to a reservation south of the Kansas River.

Other tribes such as the Kickapoo, the Iowa and the Sac and Fox occupied other parts of Indian Territory.

The biggest migration of tribes began in the early 1830s, after the U.S. Congress passed the Indian Removal Act. The **Wyandot** Indians

Shawnee

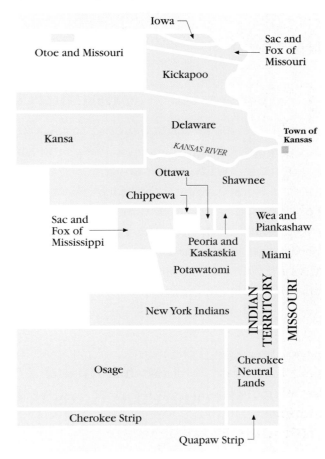

Delaware

were forced to move from Ohio by white settlers who wanted their land. They headed for Indian Territory. In 1843 the prosperous tribe bought part of what is today's **Wyandotte County** from the Delaware.

INDIAN RESERVATIONS MID-1840s

Iowa
Sac and Fox of Missouri
Otoe and Missouri
Kickapoo
Delaware
Town of Kansas
Kansa
KANSAS RIVER
Ottawa
Shawnee
Chippewa
Sac and Fox of Mississippi
Wea and Piankashaw
Peoria and Kaskaskia
Miami
Potawatomi
INDIAN TERRITORY
MISSOURI
New York Indians
Osage
Cherokee Neutral Lands
Cherokee Strip
Quapaw Strip

Missionaries

Christian missionaries arrived as the tribes did. They wanted to convert the Indians to their religion and to change the Indians' ways to be more like those of the white settlers. The tribes sometimes saw the missionaries as important in helping them deal with white settlers and with the government.

One group of Shawnee asked the Methodist church for a missionary. They got the **Rev. Thomas Johnson**, who established a mission several miles inside Indian Territory in 1830. In 1839 he moved it close to the Missouri

Johnson

Street names, county boundaries are modern-day

Kansas Avenue
KANSAS RIVER
Methodist Mission 1830-1839
WESTPORT
Baptist Mission
Methodist Mission From 1839
WYANDOTTE COUNTY
JOHNSON COUNTY
Quaker Mission
Quivira Avenue
Metcalf Avenue
MISSOURI
N
Shawnee Mission Parkway

border.

At Johnson's mission Shawnee youths were taught various skills. Also they worked in Johnson's large farming operation. Three

McCoy

buildings of this mission still stand in Fairway, Kan.

Another group of Shawnee asked for a Baptist missionary. In 1831, **Isaac McCoy** took that job. McCoy, who had also surveyed the area, joined with **Johnston Lykins** and built a mission near the edge of a ridge overlooking Turkey Creek. The first newspaper in the territory was published at the mission in the Shawnee language. It was called *Siwinowe Kesibwi,* or *Shawnee Sun.*

In 1837 the Quakers established their own mission.

Moving West

Commerce of the prairie

In 1821, just after Mexico won its independence from Spain, a trader named **William Becknell** traveled from Missouri to **Santa Fe** with goods for sale. Santa Fe was then the northernmost city of Mexico. Becknell returned to Missouri with big profits. That made Santa Fe a popular destination for many traders. The route they used became known as the Santa Fe Trail.

The original jumping-off spot was **Franklin** in east-central Missouri. Travelers and particularly traders who carried goods to sell in Santa Fe wanted to go by water as far as they could. Boats were easier and more efficient than animals or wagons.

When **Independence** was founded in 1827, its merchants established a landing on the river. Then Independence replaced Franklin as the favorite jumping-off spot for trail travelers. They could outfit themselves there with food, supplies and animals.

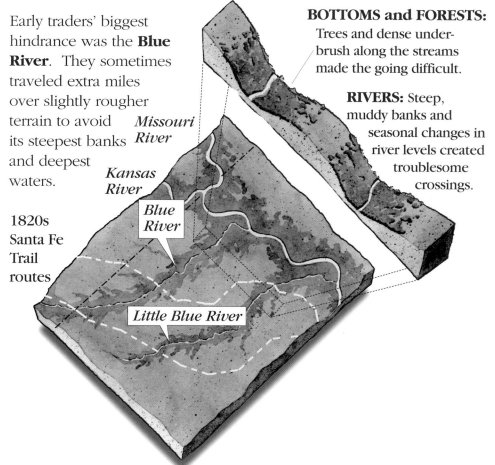

Ilustration above: A caravan arriving at the edge of Santa Fe.

The Santa Fe Trail through the Kansas City area

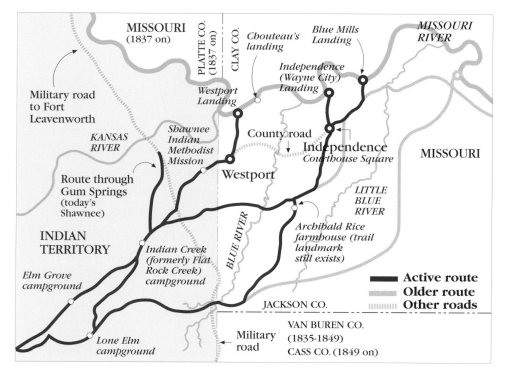

Shown in red are Santa Fe Trail routes used in the late 1820s and the 1830s. Earlier routes are shown in gray.

Blazing a trail
Freighters sought the easiest Route

Early traders' biggest hindrance was the **Blue River**. They sometimes traveled extra miles over slightly rougher terrain to avoid its steepest banks and deepest waters.

1820s Santa Fe Trail routes

BOTTOMS and FORESTS: Trees and dense underbrush along the streams made the going difficult.

RIVERS: Steep, muddy banks and seasonal changes in river levels created troublesome crossings.

Missouri River

Kansas River

Blue River

Little Blue River

Westport

The McCoys

While he was still a student in Ohio, **John Calvin McCoy** got a temporary job as a surveyor with his father on the American frontier.

Isaac McCoy, Calvin's father, had won a contract with the government to survey the Delaware lands in Indian Territory just west of Missouri. Young Calvin McCoy helped with the survey, returned to finish school in Ohio, and then moved to Jackson County, Mo. He bought some land next to his father's home along Mill Creek and opened a store in 1833.

John Calvin McCoy

The store took advantage of traffic on a road between Independence and the Indian agency in Indian Territory only a few miles to the west.

In 1834, McCoy persuaded the captain of the steamer John Hancock to land at the rock landing along the Missouri River. From there, goods were carted south along a road that led to McCoy's store. In 1835, McCoy laid out a town on his property and called it **West Port**. He improved the road between the new town, later called Westport, and the rock landing at the river.

The pioneer mother statue in Penn Valley Park honors all westward-bound women.

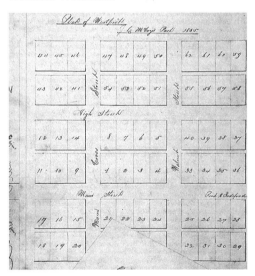

HARRIS HOUSE,
CORNER OF MAIN AND MAIN CROSS STS.,
WESTPORT, MO.
JOHN HARRIS, Proprietor.
THIS HOUSE IS LARGE COMMODIOUS AND supplied with everything necessary to the comfort and convenience of Travelers and Boarders. HACKS run regularly between this House and the river, and Stages here connect for all parts of the State and Kansas Territory. oct 15,1y

This advertisement for a Westport hotel appeared in 1858 in *The Border Star*, a weekly newspaper published in Westport. Left, a copy of Calvin McCoy's 1835 plan of Westport.

Westport's Landing

Using the river landing as its own port, Westport began to win the **Santa Fe Trail** trade from Independence. Traders who used the rock landing and the road to Westport cut about a dozen miles off the hilly, jolting overland trip from Independence. The traffic at the landing gave McCoy and other business people a new idea — start a town there.

Trade from the trails

SANTA FE and OREGON TRAILS

Both the Santa Fe and Oregon Trails crossed here, northeast to southwest, beginning 1821. The trails took separate courses farther west. A new route through Kansas Territory was opened north of here in the 1830s after the founding of Westport, Mo. Long after that became the main one, this route continued in use by pioneers and tradesmen out of Independence, Mo.

CONTRIBUTED BY OPTIMIST CLUB OF BLUE VALLEY IN COOPERATION WITH BLUE VALLEY COMMUNITY COUNCIL AND THE HISTORICAL SOCIETY OF BLUE VALLEY

In the early 1840s the opening of Oregon for settlement created more traffic for Jackson County. The **Oregon Trail** followed the Santa Fe route into Indian Territory.

In 1849 gold-hungry prospectors headed for **California** would use the same route through the area.

Santa Fe traffic, which had been restricted from 1846 to 1848 because of the United States' war with Mexico, resumed. Now, Santa Fe was in U.S. territory, and American traders no longer had to pay tariffs to Mexico.

The trade expanded enormously. Freighting companies like **Russell, Majors & Waddell** made big profits in the Kansas City area.

Oregon Trail

Kansas City

California Trail

Santa Fe Trail

A Town is Born

In 1838 a group of 14 men successfully bid on a 257-acre plot of land bordering the Missouri River. This property contained a rock landing where boats could tie up. The land had been owned by the heirs of **Gabriel Prudhomme**, a farmer who had died in a brawl in 1831.

The 14, who paid $4,220 for the property, called themselves the **Town of Kansas Co.** They were led by William Sublette, a powerful fur trader from St. Louis.

Others in the group were William Gillis, a longtime Indian trader and one of the wealthiest men in the area, and Samuel C. Owens, the principal merchant of Independence.

Also joining the group were John Calvin McCoy and his father-in-law, William Miles Chick. Chick owned a store in Westport, a warehouse along the river and a fine house on the bluffs. The rest:

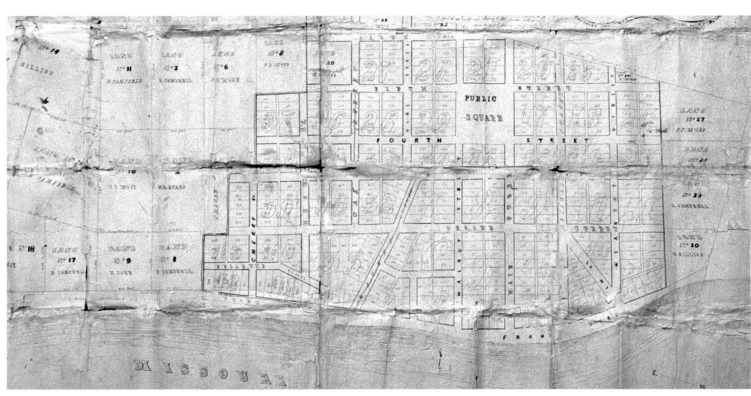

An 1847 plan or plat of the Town of Kansas.

Oliver Caldwell, William Collins, Abraham Fonda, Russell Hicks, Fry P. McGee, Jacob Ragan, James Smart, George Tate and Moses Wilson.

The Town of Kansas made little progress in the next eight years. Legal disputes and arguments among the 14 owners — some of whom died — caused the delay.

In 1846 the town got going. The owners, now reduced to seven, hired a town attorney, set aside a public square and dedicated land for a graveyard.

About the name

In early 1839 about eight of the town company gathered to discuss improving the landing, surveying the town, building a town warehouse and giving their new community a name.

They rejected "Port Fonda," named after one member of the company. They passed over scornful suggestions such as "Possumtrot" and "Rabbitville."

Finally, they selected "Kansas," after the river that flowed nearby. The river had been named for the Indian tribe that lived near it.

Early organization

Until 1850 the **Town of Kansas** amounted to a set of lots with owners but no real organization responsible for the entire unit. Its leaders wanted to assign tasks necessary for the good of all — such as peacekeeping.

So in February 1850 they asked Jackson County administrators to organize as a town. The town would be governed by a group of trustees.

The first group was rejected and the second accepted on **June 3, 1850**. The trustees elected a president and secretary from

among themselves. They appointed other positions, such as treasurer and tax collector.

Finally, a city

With the beginnings of movement for statehood in Indian Territory, leaders of the Town of Kansas aimed to establish a stronger form of government.

Leaders asked the Missouri General Assembly, and on **Feb. 22, 1853**, the **City of Kansas** officially came into being. A mayor, a marshal and six council members were elected. They levied taxes, built roads, improved the riverfront landing as a wharf for steamboats and installed a town pump for water.

Activities

IN SCHOOL

■ This chapter includes a picture of a long-ago party made by Alfred Jacob Miller. **Draw a picture of a party today.** Will you include people dancing in your party?

Compare your party scene with Alfred Jacob Miller's. Take a piece of paper and turn it horizontally. Fold your paper in half and write "Similarities" on one half and "Differences" on the other. Now write what is the same about these two party pictures and what is different.

■ **Write the word "CROSSROADS"** vertically on a piece of paper. Next to each letter, write a word or a phrase that starts with that letter describing something about Kansas City's earliest days.

■ **Look up the origin of the name "Missouri."** Write a rap music piece about the different people who have used this name.

■ **Look at Nicolas Point's line drawing** of people passing a church in 1840. Pretend that it is your job to make the engravings

or pictures for a local newspaper. **Draw a picture** of what happened 20 minutes BEFORE Father Point's drawing, and another picture of what happened 10-20 minutes AFTER. See how many people in your class can tell which is your "before" and which is your "after" illustration.

■ Refer to the illustration of the Native American tribes on Indian Territory reservations in 1846. **Research one tribe and write a paragraph** about one skill that a child your age would be taught in that tribe. Write another paragraph about one responsibility you would have if you were a part of that community. Title your work, "Children of the _____ Tribe." Illustrate your paragraphs.

WITH YOUR FAMILY

■ **Visit Missouri Town 1855** or take a trip to the **Tallgrass Prairie National Preserve** near Strong City, Kan. (It's 18 miles west of Emporia. For more information, search the World Wide Web.) The Tallgrass Prairie was the hunting grounds of the Kansa and Osage Indians in the Flint Hills. Listen to an audiotape of the book *Little House on the Prairie* while you drive and discuss what you have in common with Laura Ingalls. Did you cross Plum Creek to get there? Be sure to take a long hike and turn all of the way around, slowly. Did you see any signs of current civilization?

Missouri Town 1855.

■ **Create a simple car bingo game** using as many things as you can from *Little House on the Prairie*. Include plants, animals, and all aspects of nature in your game. Play it on your trip.

■ **Visit the Treasures of the Steamboat Arabia museum** (www.1856.com) in the city market area at 400 Grand Blvd. in Kansas City. Take a set of twelve 3x5 cards with you. Number the cards from 1-12. Distribute your cards among your family members. Explore the museum for the number of "Treasures in a Cornfield"

you have on your cards. Turn each of your cards over and either write or draw your treasures on the back of your cards. For example, if you have the number 3, look for three of the same treasure and draw or write that on the back of your card. Make a copy of each card when you get home and play a match game, or invent your own Treasure Hunters game.

■ **Visit the Shawnee Indian Mission State Historical Site** in Fairway, Kan. It is at 53rd Street and Mission Road. Create a family ABC book to record your visit. While you are there, take photos or draw pictures. When you return home, use these images to illustrate as many different letters of the alphabet as you can. Challenge another family and see who comes up with more words or phrases related to the Indian mission.

Shawnee Indian Mission State Historical Site

CHAPTER TWO

1854~1865

Brother against brother

Kansas City isn't much of a town in 1854, but this will change soon. The national argument over slavery and states' rights has divided the South and the North for decades. Suddenly, with the question of statehood for Kansas, our region becomes a central battleground for the future of the American Union.

Slaveholders in Missouri are pitted against New Englanders who are establishing towns like Quindaro, Lawrence, and Manhattan. The new arrivals hope to keep Kansas a free state and help end slavery.

The issue is loyalty to the Union. Should the United States stay together as a single country, or should states be allowed to become miniature nations? The question is settled more often in violent brawls than in polite debates. Tensions in Kansas City and the eastern part of Kansas are high, and violence is the rule of the day. Far away in Washington, Congress tries to compromise — but the battle lines have been drawn.

In the 20th century many Americans will believe that politics is dirty. They will say that politicians sometimes focus too much on personality and too little on issues.

In the years leading to the Civil War, however, personality and issues are not easy to separate. You are either for or against slavery. Your political beliefs determine whom you call a friend, whether your neighbors talk to you, and even whether the merchant on the riverfront will sell you food.

TIME TRAVELER

This is why the Civil War will be known as the war that pits brother against brother — a war that will end with more than a million Americans, nearly one of every 20 persons in the country — killed in battle.

It may be hard to imagine that people can feel so strongly about an issue that they will burn down someone's house or even kill another person. But that is what makes this the gloomiest period in American history.

Once the Civil War begins, the major battles will be fought largely east of the Mississippi River. Yet in the years before the war, the debate over the future of the United States will be played out in the Kansas City area, at the boundary between North and South, East and West. These events will occur on streets as ordinary as the ones where you live. It's not hard to imagine that these events are real. The names of the places sound familiar — Lawrence, Wyandotte, Olathe, Topeka, Westport. So do the names of the some of the villains — or heroes, depending on your point of view.

In 20th century Kansas City, in Loose Park south of the Country Club Plaza, you will see cannons commemorating a wartime battle that took place there. In Lexington, Mo., just east of Kansas City, a Civil War cannonball will still be lodged in a column at the county courthouse.

This is the real magic of history — not looking at the past in a wistful or a dreamy way — but recognizing that people in the past had to wrestle with difficult and troubling issues.

Trouble crosses the border. Then comes war

In 1854, Congress created the Kansas Territory with the idea of making it a state. Congress let residents vote on whether the state should allow slavery.

The new Kansas Territory, of course, lay only a few hundred yards west of the tiny new City of Kansas. Missourians, hoping to sway the decision toward slavery, crossed the border by the thousands. They did not want a free state nearby. Meanwhile, from eastern states came anti-slavery settlers.

The two groups clashed repeatedly, and scores of people died before anti-slavery forces won. They brought Kansas into the Union as a free state in 1861, before the Civil War began.

Along the Kansas-Missouri line, gangs on either side plundered farms and towns on the opposing side. Federal troops kept the peace inside Kansas City. Outside town, life was frightening, no matter which side you were on.

In 1864 the war came almost to Kansas City's doorstep. Just south of the town of Westport, Confederate troops clashed for two days with Union troops. The Union troops prevailed, and the Confederates retreated south. A few months later the Civil War ended, and Missouri slaves were freed.

The city's businesses and its morale were badly damaged by the war. Estimates are that its population dropped in the years 1860 to 1865.

From left: John Brown, a foe of slavery; the U.S. flag at the time of the Civil War; pro-slavery raider "Bloody" Bill Anderson; the Confederate battle flag.

Making States

The push to create a state west of Missouri came from farmers, investors and backers of a transcontinental railroad. In Congress a plan was pushed to convert Indian Territory into Nebraska Territory.

The biggest issue of the day was **slavery**, and the question quickly arose: Will **Nebraska** be slave or free? Sen. Stephen Douglas presented a compromise. Instead of creating one state, create two and let each decide the slavery question by voting.

The territory was divided, and the southern portion named **Kansas**. The northern part was Nebraska. The national government made treaties moving the Indian tribes off the land, and in **1854** the territories were opened for settlement. Counties like **Johnson** and **Leavenworth** were created in 1855 by the territorial legislature. They were among the first 33 counties established in Kansas Territory. In 1859 **Wyandotte County** was formed from parts of Johnson and **Leavenworth** counties.

The sides clash

Missourians poured across the border into Kansas Territory to vote. They elected a pro-slavery territorial Legislature. They eventually settled on **Lecompton** as their territorial capital, and their deliberations became big news all over the country.

In 1855 a growing number of anti-slavery settlers formed their own government for the territory. They met in **Topeka**.

Among the free-soilers who moved to Kansas was **John Brown**, who was fanatical in his opposition to slavery. In 1856 a band of pro-slavery men stormed **Lawrence** and plundered the town. Days later John Brown and his sons tried to avenge the Lawrence attack by stabbing or shooting to death several pro-slavery farmers along Pottawatomie Creek. That was the first of many bloody conflicts along the border.

Constitution Hall in Lecompton.

John Brown, as depicted in a mural at the Kansas Capitol.

INFORMATION
KANZAS IMMIGRANTS:

poses for many years, or until another crop can be grown."

The principal varieties of wood are bass or linwood, cottonwood, hickory, oak, black walnut, ash, sycamore, hackberry, &c.

WEATHER.—This of course cannot reasonably be expected to be uniformly the same, all years, for corresponding seasons. The same variations that are experienced elsewhere must be looked for and provided against in Kanzas; though we believe, as a general rule, the variations there will be less frequent and extreme

In from the East

Free-state partisans got off riverboats at Kansas City to make their way west. In 1856 and 1857 one riverfront hotel recorded 27,000 arrivals. Kansas City businesses profited from this activity. This drawing of the City of Kansas in 1855 was printed in Boston. Perhaps it was meant to encourage free-state supporters in New England to move to Kansas Territory. At right, a handbook told settlers what to expect.

Freedom vs. Slavery

FIFTY NEGROES,
Men, Women, Boys and Girls, Wanted
THE HIGHEST CASH PRICE will be paid for sound and healthy Negroes, to work on a farm. Apply personally or by letter to JAMES M. HUNTER,
Sept. 9-tf. Jones' Hotel, Independence.

From the *Border Star*, a weekly newspaper published in Westport, 1859.

Slavery

Missourians feared that, if Kansas entered the Union as a free state, Missouri slaves would slip away to it. In 1855 so many slaves were being stolen or had run away that Kansas City imposed a curfew. Black people, slave or free, could not be on the streets at night without a pass. By 1860 there were 4,000 slaves in Jackson County.

Free-staters prevail

late.
    SEC. 6. There shall be no slavery in this State; and no involuntary servitude, except for the punishment of crime, whereof the party shall have been duly convicted.
    SEC. 7. The right to worship G— according to the

Anti-slavery settlers won the Kansas territorial Legislature in 1857. In early 1858 they won a constitutional referendum. These were growing signs that the free-state side would win in Kansas.

In 1859 a constitutional convention met in Wyandotte, just west of Kansas City. It adopted a plan to admit Kansas into the Union as a **free state**. The plan

Kansas City Daily Western Journal of Commerce.
CITY OF KANSAS, WEDNESDAY MORNING, AUGUST 3, 1856.

CONSTITUTION
OF THE
STATE OF KANSAS;
Adopted at Wyandot, July 29, '59.
ORDINANCE.
Whereas, the Government of the United States is the proprietor of a large portion of the Lands included in the limits of the State of Kansas as defined

was sent to Congress but blocked by Southerners there. In late 1860, Abraham Lincoln was elected

The new constitution of Kansas, adopted in Wyandotte. It was printed in a Kansas City newspaper in 1859.

president, and several Southern states seceded from the Union. Then, Kansas had enough votes in Congress to win admission as a free state in **January 1861.**

The War Begins

Missouri allowed slavery, just like the Southern states that were seceding from the Union. When the Civil War began in early 1861, Union troops quickly took control of St. Louis, the state's largest city, and Jefferson City, the capital. Pro-Confederate Missouri officials were forced to flee to Texas. They became a government in exile. Even though these Confederate officials voted for Missouri to join the Confederate States of America, they had no power to enforce the decision. Missouri remained a slave state and a member of the Union.

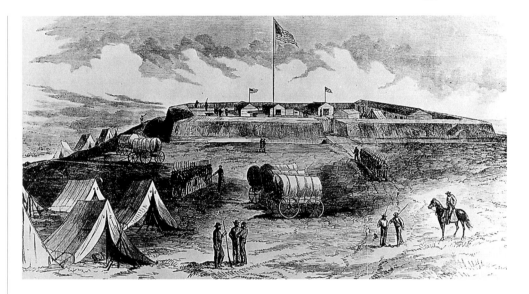

Kansas City garrison

In June 1861, only a few months after the war started, Kansas City was occupied by 200 federal soldiers. They were stationed at **Camp Union**, at 10th and Central streets, left. Despite the presence of these soldiers, the city had a sizable number of residents who openly sided with the Confederacy.

The border

Outside Kansas City, along the Kansas-Missouri border, Missouri's Southern sympathizers and Kansas' Unionists raided one another throughout the war. One side's raid would be avenged by the other. Raiders on each side burned, looted and plundered farms where they thought their opponents' sympathizers lived. Sometimes they killed male occupants. Many raiders were little more than thugs and thieves. Both sides resold for profit goods they stole in raids. Kansas raiders were called **Jayhawkers** or Red Legs. Missouri raiders were called **bushwhackers** or border ruffians.

This illustration in a Northern newspaper showed border ruffians advancing drunkenly on Kansas.

The hottest heads

Among leaders on the pro-Union side, **James Lane** of Kansas was one of the most extreme. In fall 1861 his band of raiders entered Missouri, looting and burning farms and villages. When they arrived in Osceola, they robbed the bank, looted the courthouse and rode off with vast amounts of plunder.

The most notorious leader of the pro-Southern raiders was **William Quantrill**. He led a raid on Olathe, Kan., on Sept. 2, 1862, that caught residents off guard. His guerrillas plundered the town and captured more than 100 Union soldiers.

Lane   **Quantrill**

Above: soldiers of a Kansas unit. Below: Free State Artillery Battery, Kansas.

The sound of war

Laura Coates was 8 years old when the Civil War ended. She was the daughter of two Union sympathizers, Kersey and Sarah Coates. The family home sat on Quality Hill two blocks west of Camp Union. A cannon sounded when citizens and soldiers were to report for duty. Here's how she remembered the war:

Laura

"One scene I well recall. It is the dead of night, the cannon's rumbling. ...I jump from my cot, a startled, wailing child, and run to my mother's side, but she still rocks to and fro....Her cheek is pale. I press my own against it....

"I climb up in her lap, clasp my arms around her waist and hide my face. 'Quantrell is advancing!' is the cry of every one....

"The cannon was constantly repeating the signals of alarm given by the pickets stationed on the outskirts of the city, the heart of every inhabitant quickened by the sound. Indiscriminate shooting continued among the guards, a bullet whizzing through our bedroom window one morning at the break of day....

"I have but to close my eyes to see a motley mob upon a distant hill in the present vicinity of Thirteenth and Wyandotte streets, congregated to witness a most hideous spectacle. A scaffold is outlined in the distance. The figure suspended from its beams is but partially obscured by the curious, morbid spectators. A spy is paying his death penalty!

"The next day a new-made grave is detected in a near ravine. Ever after the children hasten when obliged to pass it, and but few grown-up folk have the hardihood to go that way in the night-time."

From In Memoriam, *edited by Laura Coates Reed, 1897.*

The Heat of Battle

Crackdown

The Union commander of troops in western Missouri, **Gen. Thomas Ewing**, tried to control pro-Southern bushwhackers by controlling the people who gave them shelter — usually family members.

Among other things, Ewing imprisoned female relatives of some of the most noted bushwhacker leaders. He accused them of being spies who provided valuable information to the pro-Confederate raiders.

On Aug. 13, 1863, the three-story building housing their makeshift jail on Grand Avenue **collapsed**. Four of the nine women prisoners died.

An eastern newspaper artist created this depiction of Quantrill's raid.

Raid on Lawrence

Quantrill and his allies were infuriated by Ewing's orders and by the death of their kin in the Kansas City jail. They decided to raid **Lawrence, Kan.**, which was ardently pro-Union. Lawrence residents helped supply many of the Kansas raiders who were striking Missouri. Quantrill and 450 men started the 50-mile ride to Lawrence on the night of Aug. 20, 1863. Early the next morning — **Aug. 21, 1863** — they struck the town, which was undefended. They killed 150 men and boys. They harmed no women, but they left scores of widows, and left much of Lawrence in flames. They carried away loot by the wagonload.

Order No. 11

Ewing responded to the Lawrence raid four days later. He issued his **General Order No. 11**, requiring evacuation of most Missourians living in the counties along the Kansas border. Twenty thousand people were forced to leave the area and find new homes. Union soldiers often burned the buildings that these refugees abandoned. Those living in Kansas City and a few other towns were exempted. The artist **George Caleb Bingham**, a Missourian, was so affected by Order No. 11 that he created this dramatic painting intended to create outrage at Ewing.

Fighting in KC

Full battle

About 10,000 Confederate troops entered Missouri from Arkansas in late summer 1864. Their commander, **Gen. Sterling Price**, aimed to attack Union forces in St.

Price

Louis. He hoped that this would draw the Union's attention from the Civil War in Virginia and so help Gen. Robert E. Lee's forces there. Price attacked a Union stronghold in southeast Missouri, Pilot Knob, but the federal defenders escaped. He advanced north toward St. Louis but found the city too strongly defended by Union troops. Then he headed west. After being repulsed by Union troops at Jefferson City, Price aimed to attack Kansas City and Fort Leavenworth. Meanwhile, Union forces chased him from behind.

Battle of Westport

In late October 1864, Price's troops pushed through Independence, drove Union defenders back from the **Blue River** and on Oct. 22 camped south of **Brush Creek**, across from **Westport**. The morning of Oct. 23 the Confederates attacked, but the Union forces held and drove the Confederates back. When reports arrived that other Union forces were attacking from the east, Price retreated south to avoid being trapped. The Confederates headed south along the Missouri-Kansas border and back to Arkansas.

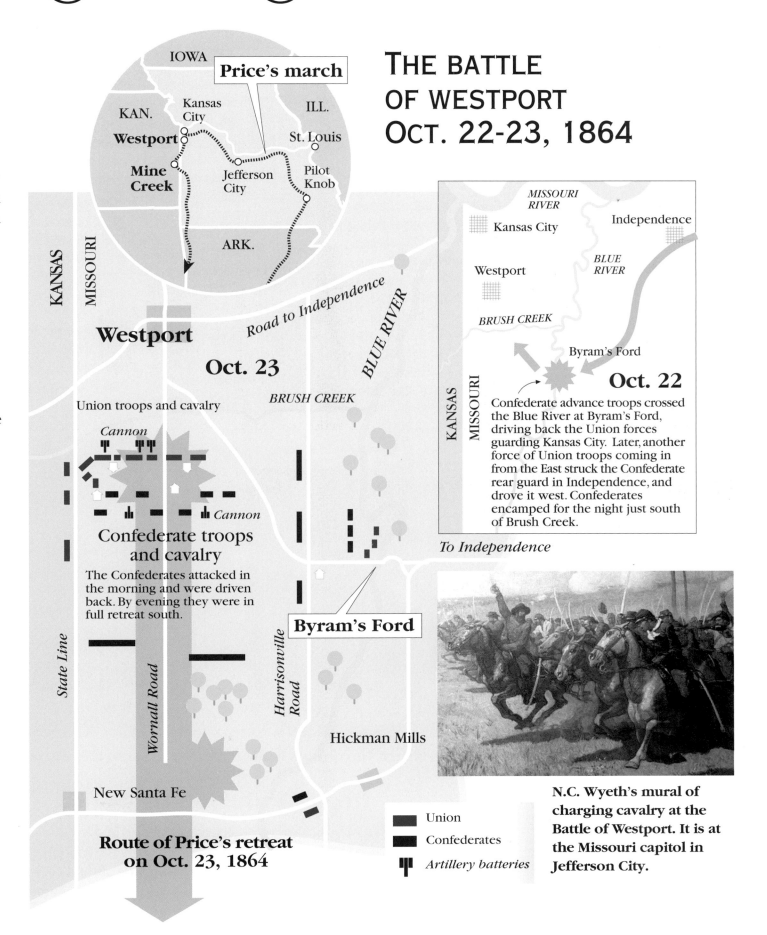

THE BATTLE OF WESTPORT OCT. 22-23, 1864

Price's march

IOWA
KAN.
Kansas City
ILL.
Westport
St. Louis
Mine Creek
Jefferson City
Pilot Knob
ARK.

KANSAS
MISSOURI

Westport
Oct. 23

Road to Independence

BLUE RIVER

BRUSH CREEK

Union troops and cavalry

Cannon

Cannon

Confederate troops and cavalry

The Confederates attacked in the morning and were driven back. By evening they were in full retreat south.

Byram's Ford

State Line

Wornall Road

Harrisonville Road

Hickman Mills

New Santa Fe

Route of Price's retreat on Oct. 23, 1864

MISSOURI RIVER

Kansas City
Independence

Westport
BLUE RIVER

BRUSH CREEK

KANSAS
MISSOURI

Byram's Ford

Oct. 22

Confederate advance troops crossed the Blue River at Byram's Ford, driving back the Union forces guarding Kansas City. Later, another force of Union troops coming in from the East struck the Confederate rear guard in Independence, and drove it west. Confederates encamped for the night just south of Brush Creek.

To Independence

N.C. Wyeth's mural of charging cavalry at the Battle of Westport. It is at the Missouri capitol in Jefferson City.

Union
Confederates
Artillery batteries

Aftermath

Hard times as the war wears on

The Union victory at the Battle of Westport did not halt guerrilla raids in the area. They would be curbed only by the end of the Civil War six months later.

Four years of this activity badly damaged commerce in the area. Union soldiers were assigned to provide relief to Kansas City's growing number of poor and hungry residents. Their commander acknowledged, however, that not everyone could be helped.

Confederate forces in the east surrendered to Union forces in **April 1865**, bringing the Civil War to an end except in scattered areas of the west. The surrender came none too soon for Kansas City, which had suffered four years of misery.

Veterans of both sides in the battle of Westport gathered for reunions in the 1920s. In this photo they are standing in front of the Westport library.

Hope for the future

Railroads began building new tracks in the Kansas City area even before the war ended. **Wyandotte**, Kan., was connected by rail to Lawrence (the trip took 3 and one-half hours). In September the **Missouri Pacific** railroad was completed from St. Louis to Kansas City south of the Missouri River. Yet there was no bridge at St. Louis for travelers and freight headed to Chicago and to Eastern markets. The **Hannibal & St. Joseph** had completed a line across the northern part of the state, but getting to it required ferrying across the Missouri River and taking a stagecoach to Weston. Kansas Citians now began to wish for a rail connection all the way to the big cities of the East.

Activities

■ **Write each of these events on a different index card** or strip of paper. Write the dates on the back in pencil.

* Topeka, Kan., formed by anti-slavery settlers (1855)
* Civil War ends (1865)
* Battle of Westport (1864)
* Lawrence, Kan., plundered by pro-slavery forces (1856 and 1863)
* John Brown kills several pro-slavery farmers (1856)
* Missouri becomes a state (1821)
* Civil War begins (1861)
* Kansas enters union as free state (1861)
* Curfew imposed on Kansas City slaves (1855)
* Congress creates Kansas Territory (1854)
* Lincoln elected president (1860)

Divide the class into two groups. Time each group as its members, without looking at the date on the back, try to arrange these events in the correct date order on the floor. Which team had the most dates in the correct order? Now tape these along a time line in the hallway or on the floor of the classroom. Illustrate the time line.

■ **Stage a classroom debate:** the Jayhawkers vs. the Bushwhackers. What Civil War topic will you argue? Invite parents, Youthfriend volunteers or the principal to come in and judge your event.

■ **Print these imaginary newspaper headlines** on separate pieces of paper:

* John Brown Slays Innocent Farmers
* Border Wars with No End in Sight
* War Between the States Is Imminent
* Jayhawkers Have Right Idea
* Free State or Nothing: Kansas Won't Budge
* Slaveholding: A Proud Tradition
* Anti-Slavery Settlers Prevail in Kansas Legislature
* Several Southern States Secede from the Union

Write "Fact" and "Opinion" on the board and categorize these headlines with a partner. Using a headline you have chosen, write "the rest of the story."

■ **Create your own headline** for a front-page article announcing the end of the Civil War.

■ **Design a poster** highlighting one of the freedoms you have today that a student living in the 19th century would not have had.

The spring and cave at Cave Spring in Kansas City.

■ **Search *The Kansas City Star*** and listen to the news for countries involved in civil wars or disputes. What are the main issues dividing countries today? Do you ever argue about these issues in your family?

The Bingham-Waggoner Estate.

■ **Visit one of these historic homes:**
* John Wornall House Museum, 146 W. 61st Terrace, Kansas City
* Alexander Majors Historical House, 8201 State Line Road, Kansas City
* Bingham-Waggoner Estate, 313 W. Pacific Ave., Independence

■ **Make a 12x18 drawing** of the outside of the building and draw your family in front of the house. Will you be dressed in clothes of today, or of the period appropriate to the home? Have your drawings laminated and use them as place mats in your home.

■ **Hike the trails** at the Cave Spring Interpretive Center at 8701 E. Gregory Blvd. in Kansas City. What have these springs been used for in the past? Come home and play checkers or make your own paper doll or game that relates to something from the 1800s.

■ **Watch the newspaper** and check out Web sites for activities taking place along Brush Creek. Attend an event with your family and write a paragraph about it for a family journal. Ask your parents or grandparents what the creek used to look like when they were your age. Did they ever walk along it?

CHAPTER THREE

1866~1893

The city takes off

If you are the mayor of Kansas City after the Civil War, what will you do to make sure that your town will grow to be a large city?

This is the central question facing Kansas City leaders as they try to shake off the war's aftermath. As the war ends, only a few hundred people remain in this riverfront community.

There is no particular reason to believe that Kansas City ever will amount to much. Or is there?

Kansas City is the product of promoters, people who know that their livelihood depends on convincing others that the little town on the bluffs is a good place to live. These boosters, as they are known, quickly dust off plans that have been sitting idle for nearly 10 years.

Build a railroad, they say. Not just any railroad. Build the greatest railroad in the Midwest. Connect Kansas City to a great central railroad extending north to the Great Lakes, and south to the Gulf of Mexico. But there's one major problem. Building such a railroad means that the greatest feature on the landscape — the Missouri River — must be crossed.

The railroads must be convinced that Kansas City is the ideal site for a bridge. Not just any bridge, but a bridge crossing one of the surliest and swiftest rivers in the United States.

Kansas City boosters have bragged that a great city is destined to rise where the Kansas River joins the Missouri. First, however, the landscape must be conquered.

To do that, Kansas Citians will call on the mind of one of America's greatest engineers, Octave Chanute. He designed the Chicago Stockyards and one day will help the Wright Brothers invent the airplane. Kansas Citians also will call on the muscles and sweat of hundreds of workers. Together these people will build the Kansas City bridge.

The story of the bridge is the story of Kansas City's genesis, the story of how a great city finally came to be. The bridge will link Kansas City to the railroads of Chicago and the East Coast. It will ensure a steady stream of goods, visitors, new residents, and talented and eager young people for the growing city.

Despite all this progress in the decades after the bridge opens, Kansas City will remain a rough-and-tumble place. Even by the early 1890s the city's beauty will exist more in the imagination of its founders than in the reality of its daily life. The magnificent rail yards, the shoppers promenading on downtown streets, even the rattle and clang of the busy cable cars will not hide one fact: Kansas City will still be a difficult and dangerous place for many people.

First comes a bridge

Before the Civil War, Leavenworth and St. Joseph were about twice as large as Kansas City. When the war ended, these neighbors up the Missouri River were four times as large. Because of Kansas City's perilous position at the center of border violence, business and people had left town. Leavenworth and St. Joseph were booming, and Kansas City was falling farther behind them. It could barely keep pace with Atchison, Kan.

But then Kansas City beat all its rivals in a very important contest. Kansas City won the first permanent railroad bridge across the Missouri River. Tons of products could be easily shipped through Kansas City straight to big markets. That would mean big money for Kansas City.

Ninth and Main streets, 1870s.

The bridge was opened in 1869 amid a great city celebration. Soon stockyards were built in the West Bottoms on the Kansas side of the state line. Packinghouses were built to slaughter hogs and cattle that came through town. Other factories prepared the "byproducts" of animal slaughter — soap, glue and lard. Grain elevators stored farm products, mills ground grain, and bakeries made bread and crackers. Kansas City's position in the Midwest meant that products such as food, lumber, furniture and farm machinery could be shipped rapidly to the East and eventually in all directions.

Only a few years after being down and out, Kansas City was on its way up — and rapidly. As it grew, the city became a wild frontier town. Cowboys who had brought cattle to town took

Left: Kansas City was still a rough frontier town in the late 1860s. This picture was made on Main Street. Right: By the 1890s it was a busy manufacturing center. This view shows the West Bottoms.

themselves to Kansas City saloons and gambling halls.

Meanwhile, builders carved the city right out of the mud and rock bluffs. In a few years the bluffs began to disappear. Buildings sprang up farther south, and the center of activity moved that direction. Theaters sprang up, and famous entertainers

came through town. Union Depot was opened not far from the stockyards, and soon it was jammed with travelers.

By the 1880s great new buildings were on the drawing boards for Kansas City. A new city — Kansas City, Kan. — appeared in 1886. Several Wyandotte County towns combined to form it.

The entire area was not only growing but also entering a new technological age. Kansas City got telephones and electric lights. The electric sewing machine increased the output of the city's garment makers. Cable cars began operating in 1885.

The city was set for decades of stunning growth.

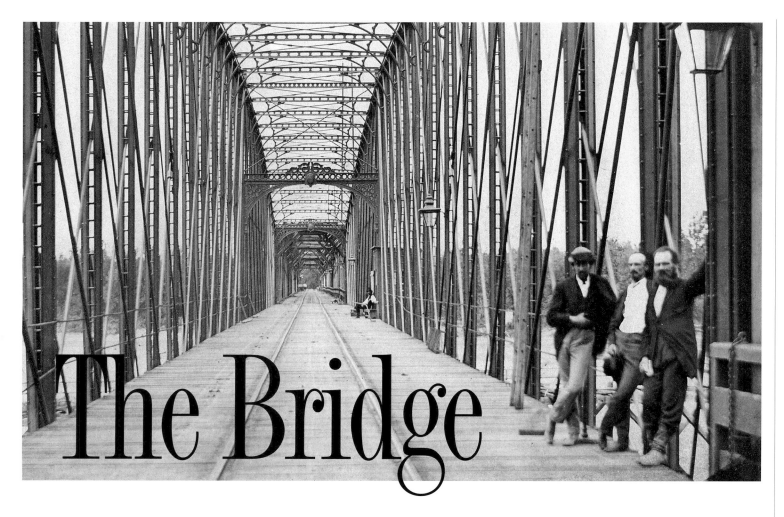

The Bridge

Once the Civil War ended, railroads returned to laying track, much of it west of the Mississippi River. Kansas City was reached by the Missouri Pacific in 1865. Yet the Missouri River remained an obstacle. A permanent bridge had to be built somewhere to cross the river, and many cities wanted it. The city that lay at the crossing would no doubt experience a boom.

Kansas City boosters went to work. **Robert Van Horn** and **Kersey Coates** had been promoting a railroad across the Missouri since 1857. A local lawyer, Charles Kearney, sold land he owned in the West Bottoms to James F. Joy of Detroit. Joy was a powerful executive of the **Hannibal & St. Joseph** and other lines. If Joy decided to bridge the Missouri at Kansas City, his new land would skyrocket in value.

In June 1866, **Leavenworth** leaders were making a strong case to Hannibal & St. Joseph investors in Boston to make their city the crossing point. Three prominent Kansas Citians hurried there to

A steamboat provided supplies and power for the bridge builders.

change their minds. They were James W. Reid, Theodore Case and Coates. They succeeded.

Right away they instructed Van Horn, now Kansas City's representative in the U.S.

Congress, to introduce a measure to authorize building the bridge at Kansas City. The bill also authorized the railroads to bridge the Mississippi at Quincy, Ill. The measure passed, and the railroads were pleased. Kansas City had won the race for the bridge.

From Kansas City the rail route would run northeast to Cameron, Mo. There it would meet the east-west tracks of the Hannibal & St. Joseph.

The bridge would provide an all-rail route from the West and the Southwest to the huge markets of Chicago and Eastern cities. And the route would pass right through Kansas City.

A tough job

Octave Chanute, a civil engineer born in France, was selected by the railroad to design the Kansas City bridge over the Missouri River. The task was difficult. Although the Missouri River was not as wide as the Mississippi, it was unpredictable. Often it changed course. Frequently it changed its banks. Sand shifted constantly on the river bottom, piling up and then quickly being swept away.

Chanute

Construction began in 1867. Chanute built seven stone and concrete piers to support the bridge. Four piers descended to a layer of rock. Three sat on piles driven into sandy sediment. Watertight wooden enclosures had to be constructed in the river and lowered through sand to rock. Then concrete was poured in and finally stone was set.

By summer 1869 the bridge was ready to carry trains. Chanute stayed busy in the Kansas City area. Among other things, he:

■ Designed the new stockyards.

■ Laid out a plan for the Town of Lenexa.

■ Mapped rail lines into Kansas for the Atchison, Topeka & Santa Fe Railroad and the Kansas, Fort Scott and Memphis Railroad.

He won even greater fame in other places. His research into elevated railways helped form New York's transit system. His tests on gliders and other flying devices helped the Wright Brothers build their airplane.

Chanute died in 1910 in Chicago.

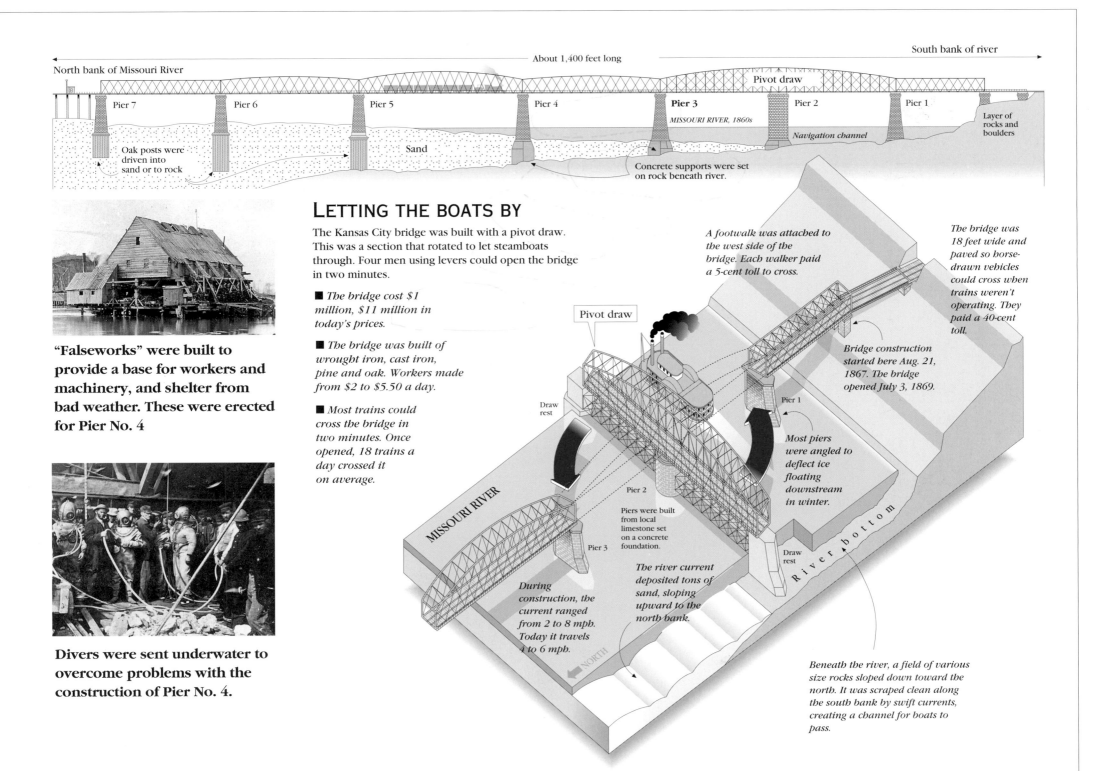

North bank of Missouri River

About 1,400 feet long

South bank of river

Pivot draw

MISSOURI RIVER, 1860s

| Pier 7 | Pier 6 | Pier 5 | Pier 4 | Pier 3 | Pier 2 | Pier 1 |

Layer of rocks and boulders

Oak posts were driven into sand or to rock

Sand

Navigation channel

Concrete supports were set on rock beneath river.

"Falseworks" were built to provide a base for workers and machinery, and shelter from bad weather. These were erected for Pier No. 4

Divers were sent underwater to overcome problems with the construction of Pier No. 4.

LETTING THE BOATS BY

The Kansas City bridge was built with a pivot draw. This was a section that rotated to let steamboats through. Four men using levers could open the bridge in two minutes.

■ *The bridge cost $1 million, $11 million in today's prices.*

■ *The bridge was built of wrought iron, cast iron, pine and oak. Workers made from $2 to $5.50 a day.*

■ *Most trains could cross the bridge in two minutes. Once opened, 18 trains a day crossed it on average.*

A footwalk was attached to the west side of the bridge. Each walker paid a 5-cent toll to cross.

The bridge was 18 feet wide and paved so horse-drawn vehicles could cross when trains weren't operating. They paid a 40-cent toll.

Pivot draw

Draw rest

Pier 1

Bridge construction started here Aug. 21, 1867. The bridge opened July 3, 1869.

MISSOURI RIVER

Pier 2

Pier 3

Piers were built from local limestone set on a concrete foundation.

Most piers were angled to deflect ice floating downstream in winter.

Draw rest

River bottom

During construction, the current ranged from 2 to 8 mph. Today it travels 4 to 6 mph.

The river current deposited tons of sand, sloping upward to the north bank.

Beneath the river, a field of various size rocks sloped down toward the north. It was scraped clean along the south bank by swift currents, creating a channel for boats to pass.

NORTH

The celebration

On **July 3, 1869**, the residents of Kansas City flocked to the riverfront to watch the first train cross the new bridge. A hot-air balloon floated in the sky. A brass band led a parade. That night a joyous banquet was held at the Broadway Hotel. In years to come, the bridge would become known as the Hannibal Bridge.

Opening-day crowd at the bridge.

Boom!

In the first year of operation of the new bridge, an estimated quarter-million travelers passed through Kansas City, 70,000 of them by train. By 1870 the population of the city had soared to at least **25,000**. Official census records, thought by some historians to have been too high, showed 32,000. A lot on Main Street worth $400 in 1856 sold for $11,000 in 1871.

The Kansas City area in 1865

This map of Missouri and Kansas, published by A. J. Johnson in 1865, shows the Kansas City region at the end of the Civil War. Kansas City and Westport are still small, separate cities. Today's Shawnee is labeled "Shawneetown." Quindaro is still shown as a separate town.

The Livestock Arrive

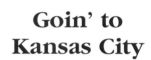

Western Kansas cowboy.

In the 1860s, ranchers in Texas were raising vast herds of cattle but had no way to get them to market. An Illinois cattle trader named **Joseph G. McCoy** came up with a plan. He went west along the newly built Kansas Pacific Railroad into Kansas. In 1867, McCoy built stock pens in Abilene. Then he advertised them across the Southwest. Soon herds of longhorn cattle were crossing Kansas to reach Abilene, where the railroad ended. From there the cattle could travel by rail to packinghouses in Chicago. Ranchers would have a market for beef.

Kansas City set up stock pens to feed and water those cattle along the way. That's how the **Kansas City stockyards** began. Soon, Kansas City became a destination instead of merely a way station. Packinghouses sprang up, and livestock traders arrived to make deals on cattle, hogs and other animals. Traders bought arriving animals and sold them to butchers, packinghouses and exporters.

Goin' to Kansas City

Money being made in the stockyards drew bankers and land buyers. The plentiful rail lines made shipping easy to all points. Farm-implement dealers established operations. Various manufacturers set up shop, using Kansas City as a base for a national market.

Wealthy Easterners who had provided much of the money for the railroads and stockyards stayed in the center of activity, heading the **Kansas City Livestock Exchange**. The development of **Armourdale**, Kan., was one of their projects.

Meatpackers

A Chicago meat packing family, the **Armours**, started the first large packinghouse in the West Bottoms in 1870. In the early years, meat packers served a largely local market. Once hogs and cattle were slaughtered, the meat could go bad before it could arrive in faraway cities. But by 1877 **refrigerated** rail cars overcame this problem. Kansas City that year shipped nearly 9 million pounds of fresh, dressed beef to Eastern cities.

Workers inside a Kansas City packing plant.

Sarah and Kersey Coates (right) with daughter Laura (lower left) entertained friends and family at their home on Quality Hill, where many of Kansas City's wealthy families lived in the 1870s.

Settling Down

Exodusters

Kansas held a special place in the hearts of black Southerners. It had been a hotbed for abolitionists and had voted to enter the Union as a free state. After the end of Reconstruction — when federal troops were withdrawn from the South and black people there began to worry about their future — thousands of black people headed for Kansas. In 1879 steamboats going up the Mississippi and the Missouri rivers were laden with former slaves. Some were attracted by false promises of free land in Kansas.

They arrived at Wyandotte, Kan., just across the state line from Kansas City. Some of these "Exodusters" received train fare to travel on west, but many settled in Wyandotte. A settlement called **Juniper Town** and later **Mississippi Town** grew along the river bottoms. Nearby, another settlement was called **Rattlebone Hollow.**

Benjamin "Pap" Singleton was a leader of the black migration to Kansas.

Schools

Kansas City opened its **first public school** in 1868. Before then children were taught at home or in private schools. The first school, above, was at Cherry Street and Independence Avenue and eventually was named **Washington School**, after the first president.

Wheat and bread

Mennonite farmers arrived in Kansas from Russia in the 1870s and began planting their own special kind of wheat, called **Turkey Red**. The wheat thrived on the Plains, much of it headed for Kansas City. Sales of grain in Kansas City ballooned tenfold. By 1880 seven grain elevators had arisen. They could store 1.5 million bushels for local mills.

Other grain was shipped on to other cities. Eventually the **Kansas City Board of Trade** became the world's busiest trading house for the red winter wheat.

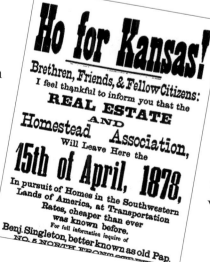

Ho for Kansas!

Brethren, Friends, & Fellow Citizens:
I feel thankful to inform you that the
REAL ESTATE
AND
Homestead Association,
Will Leave Here the
15th of April, 1878,
In pursuit of Homes in the Southwestern Lands of America, at Transportation Rates, cheaper than ever was known before.
For full information inquire of
Benj. Singleton, better known as old Pap,
NO. 5 NORTH FRONT STREET.

The way a bird would see Kansas City, in the late 1870s

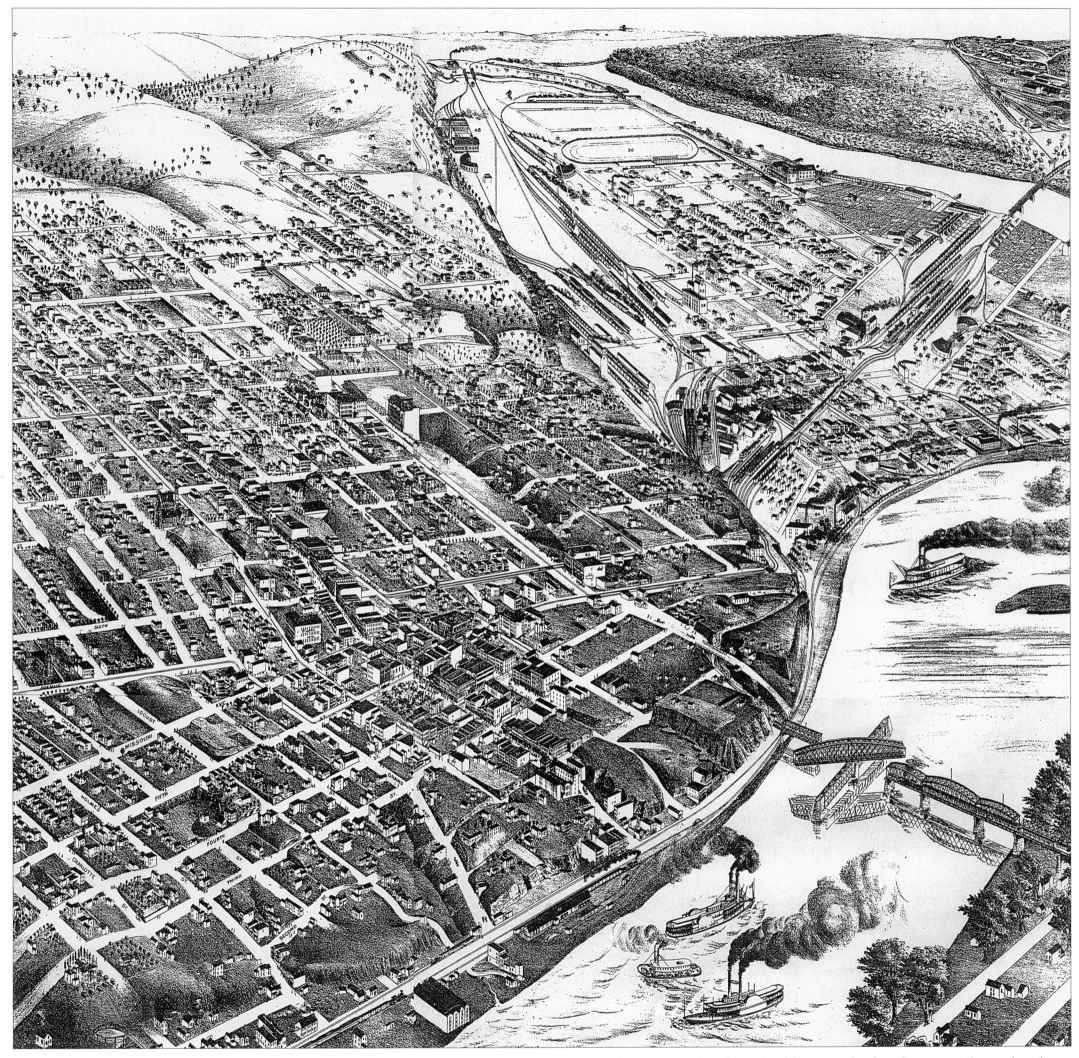

This "bird's-eye" map of Kansas City in the late 1870s was drawn by artists who walked the streets, sketching buildings and other features. These sketches were assembled into one big aerial view of the city. Compare this with the drawing on page 10.

Rowdy Times

The James gang

The fame of **Jesse** and **Frank James** began in 1866, when the former Civil War ruffians robbed a bank on the town square in **Liberty**. In the 1870s, authorities linked the gang to nearly two dozen robberies. One of them, in 1872 at the Kansas City fairgrounds, was labeled "Most Desperate and Daring Robbery of the Age" by *The Kansas City Times*. One of the Jameses' havens was their farm near **Kearney** in Clay County. Jesse James was shot to death in 1882 in St. Joseph. Frank James died in 1915 at the Clay County farm.

Jesse James

Frederic Remington

Frederic Remington, who would become perhaps the most famous artist of the Old West, lived in Kansas City in 1884 and 1885. He was a New Yorker who was trying life on the frontier. With money borrowed from his parents, he opened a hardware store. Later he became part-owner of a saloon, where he liked to sketch the patrons. He sold some early paintings through an art-supply dealer in Kansas City. After his saloon failed, he returned to New York.

As Kansas City grew, it drew large numbers of young people, particularly men, willing to take risks. For every 100 women in Jackson County in 1870 there were 122 men . These new residents often carried guns and gambled and drank through the night. Real-estate speculators made huge sums and lost them in days.

In 1878 *The Kansas City Times* recalled that the town contained "as fine a collection of ruffian brotherhood and sisterhood of the wild West as could well be imagined. Renegade Indians, demoralized soldiers, unreformed bushwhackers and border ruffians, thieves and thugs imported from anywhere, professional train robbers of home growth, and all kinds of wrecks from the Civil War."

Wild Bill Hickok

The famous gunslinger frequently visited the gambling halls and saloons on Main Street from the late 1860s through the mid-1870s.

Gullytown

Kansas Citians occasionally referred to their home as "**Gullytown**" even before the Civil War. Afterward the nickname became even more appropriate. The bluffs along the Missouri River had natural ravines and gullys already. When construction crews began cutting streets through the bluffs, the gullys became enormous. Later the hills between the streets were removed. Today, Kansas City's riverfront has a far gentler slope than it had in the 1860s.

Top left, Wyandotte Street near Third Street. Above, Kansas City's riverfront from the north. Below left, Second Street looking east toward Main Street. Below right, Seventh Street and Grand Avenue.

Newer, bigger

Investors rushed to make money in the booming city in the 1880s and grand new buildings were built:

■ **1. Exposition Hall,** finished in 1887. This structure was roofed with 80,000 square feet of glass. It housed exhibits for the Kansas City Industrial Exposition, an annual fair that began in 1871. The hall stood at 15th Street, now Truman Road, and Bellefontaine Avenue. In 1893 the fair ended. The glass roof later was shattered in a hailstorm, and the unused building was destroyed by fire in 1901.

■ **2. New York Life Building,** finished in 1890. Built to house offices of an insurance company, this building still stands at 20 W. Ninth St.

■ **3. New England Building,** finished in 1888. This structure at Ninth and Wyandotte streets still stands.

■ **4. Board of Trade Building,** finished in 1888. This building at 210 W. Eighth St. was considered to be an excellent example of architecture. It was the second permanent home of the Kansas City grain-trading business. It was torn down in 1968.

■ **5. Bullene, Moore, Emery & Co.,** finished in 1890. This department store, which became Emery, Bird, Thayer, was famed for decades until it closed in the 1960s. The building, which stretched along 11th Street between Walnut Street and Grand Avenue, was demolished in the early 1970s.

Building BOOM

Taking the train

A group of railroads wishing to combine some of their passenger and baggage services built **Union Depot,** left and above, in 1878. The ornate structure was the greatest building in the city at the time and briefly Kansas Citians were quite proud of it. But Union Depot was built for a city of 60,000. In the 1880s Kansas City shot past that. By 1890 the combined population of Kansas City and Kansas City, Kan., was more than 180,000. The depot had quickly become too crowded. Smoke from the steam engines and the nearby packing plants had given it a layer of soot and filth. Complaints were rising, but not until the late 1890s would the railroads give serious thought to a new station.

Getting Around

The fastest, cheapest way to travel on land was by rails. Trains took passengers from city to city. Streetcars moved them from block to block.

Cable cars

In 1885 miles of streets were torn up for cable-car tracks. These streetcars were powered by a moving metal cable, which ran underground. They replaced many of the streetcars drawn by horses and mules. Drivers activated a grip, which extended through a slot between the tracks to grab the always-moving cable. These cars were well-suited to Kansas City's hilly streets. One of the steepest cable-car routes was the **Ninth Street Incline**, above. It took passengers to Union Depot.

Left: Ninth and Main streets, called the Junction.

What's HOT

Electric lights

The first time **electricity** was used indoors in Kansas City came in March 1881 at the G.Y. Smith & Co. dry goods store. The lights were on from 7 p.m. to 10 p.m., and curious crowds wandered through the store at 712-716 Main St. Observers called it "the splendid triumph" of science. Within a year 13 stores in the same block had electricity.

OPENING DISPLAY

WITH THE

ELECTRIC LIGHT!

(Favorable weather permitting)

The public are very cordially invited to witness our grand display on WEDNESDAY EVENING next, weather permitting, when our entire first floor will be illuminated by the Brush Electric Light, and every department beautifully decorated.

———

SUITS AND WRAPS.

A big-league town

Kansas City's first major-league baseball team was the **Cowboys**. The team played in the National League in 1886 and in the American Association, then one of the major leagues, in 1888 and 1889. The Cowboys were unprofitable, though, and Kansas City baseball was played in the minor leagues for years afterward.

Puff! Pant!

Kansas City public schools introduced **physical education** classes in 1885, a radical idea at the time. The schools also helped students with poor eyesight get glasses. But schools were demanding, too. Precise penmanship was expected. In 1887 the district recorded 422 cases of **corporal punishment** — spanking, hitting or whipping — an average of about two by each teacher.

Boys in a gym class.

Telephones

The city's first **telephone directory** was printed in 1879. It listed 58 telephones in Kansas City. To place a call, you turned a crank to alert "central" and told the operator the number you wanted. **The Coates House**, for example, was No. 17.

Priests of Pallas

In 1887 a group of businessmen founded the **Priests of Pallas** parade. They hoped it would be a showy, annual celebration that would draw

visitors and their money to Kansas City. That year's parade featured masked drummers and giant horse-drawn floats. There was a "high priest" riding an elephant and a woman posing as the Greek goddess of wisdom. In later years the event became a weeklong party. Each year had a new theme, and the parade grew and prospered until after the turn of the century.

MEDIA

A new newspaper

A young road contractor and newspaper owner from Indiana went looking for a growing city to start a newspaper and make some money. He settled on Kansas City, and on Sept. 18, 1880, he produced the first copy of **The Kansas City Star.** The young man was **William Rockhill Nelson**, and his *Star* would outlast all its competition — *The Journal, The Times* and *The Mail*. They cost a nickel a copy. Nelson charged only 2 cents for *The Star*. In time *The Star* would become one of the hardiest and most controversial institutions in the city.

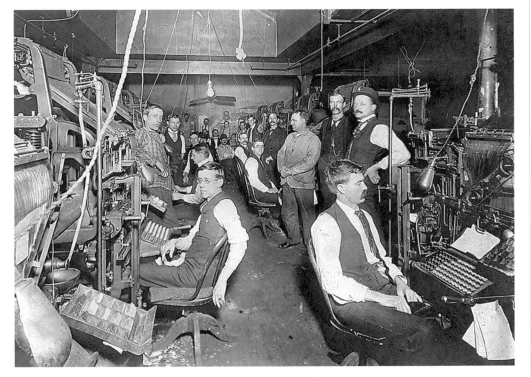

Typesetters at *The Star* around the turn of the century.

VISITORS

The President is here!

Cleveland at the federal building, Ninth and Walnut streets.

The first president to visit Kansas City while in office, **Grover Cleveland**, came to town Oct. 12, 1887, as part of a national tour with his new wife, **Frances Folsom Cleveland**. That night and the next day he made appearances at the federal building and elsewhere, and then left for Memphis, Tenn.

In Kansas City, nature often has dealt unexpected blows. In April 1881, the Missouri River flooded, driving people from homes and workers from meatpacking plants. In 1883, a tornado tore a path across downtown. Four persons were killed.

And on the morning of May 11, 1886, an even deadlier tornado struck. First, it ripped through the Missouri River railroad bridge. Then it tore the top off the **Jackson County Courthouse**.

Worst of all, the tornado struck the bell tower of the **Lathrop school**. The bell and tower collapsed inward and 15 elementary schoolchildren died inside.

One 14-year-old pupil, Jim Boro, recalled years later:

"I was panic stricken, you might say. I just had time to duck my head when that big bell came through."

Ten other persons died elsewhere in the city.

After this event, the school board removed all bell towers from schools.

Hours after the 1886 tornado struck the Lathrop School, onlookers crowded around as the bodies of children were carried away. The school stood at the corner of Eighth and May streets.

Frank Askew was a seventh-grade monitor at the Lathrop School in 1886. It was his job to ring the bell for recesses and the end of school. Fifty years after the disaster, he recalled the storm this way:

"It was so dark we could not read the blackboards and could make out the faces of pupils across the room only dimly. We could hear the rain pouring on the roof....

"Someone noticed the bell tower swaying and an effort was made to get the children out of the school. ...There came a terrific splintering and crashing. I crawled out and jumped, just as the floor sagged and started to give way. The storm had torn away the bell tower, spun it in the air and then dropped it gable foremost upon our room.

"As we watched, the ceiling bulged down. I have the awful recollection of those children throwing up their hands and starting for the door when that whole mass from the upper room fell through and enveloped them. Then the floor gave way, carrying children, timber and masonry into the basement. Fifteen were killed. It was the most terrible day of my life."

The Jackson County Courthouse at the northeast corner of Second and Main streets, before and after the tornado of 1886.

Activities

■ **Build a bridge** in your classroom with straws or toothpicks. How long can you make it before it collapses?

■ **Measure an 18-foot-wide strip of floor** in the gym or in an area of the playground and mark it off with masking tape. This is the width of the first bridge over the Missouri River in Kansas City. How many students can stand shoulder to shoulder in this space? How many cars do you think could drive side by side down this bridge? Could you have thrown a ball from one side of this bridge to the other? Create a class list of other things that measure approximately 18 feet.

■ **Create an imaginary postcard** of the first bridge crossing the Missouri River. Write about what it was like to watch the first train cross it. Date it July 3, 1869, and postmark it from Kansas City. To whom will you address it?

■ **Finish this sentence** with a story paragraph about life in the town of Wyandotte, Kan., immediately after the Civil War. "I was so happy the night my brothers and sisters arrived in Rattlebone Hollow with our . . ."

■ **You are the keeper of an inn** during the 1880s in Kansas City. You decide to get creative with your menu and offer Gully Goulash and Ruffian Ragout. Look up what these words mean, and then write a recipe for each of them. Describe the final dish for your menu.

■ Kansas City experienced a building boom after the Civil War. As a class, **go outside and find the cornerstone of your school building.** What year is on it? Stand by the cornerstone and begin naming different materials and tools used to make your school. See if you can get all of the way around the class without repeating something.

■ **Pretend you and your family own a general store** today that is designed to take people back 150 years. What will you call your company? Make an inventory of goods and services you will provide — for a price — to Kansas Citians of this century for a taste of Kansas Town in the 19th century. Will you offer daguerreotype or tintype photographic portraits of the whole family? What about dry goods?

■ **Ride the Amtrak** from Kansas City to Lawrence, Kan. What path do you seem to be following? As you go through the West Bottoms, count the different railroad lines you pass, and when you get out in the countryside, list the different species of animals you observe. Interview the conductor and ask about the most unusual animal he or she has ever spotted along these tracks.

■ **Visit the American Royal Museum** and Visitors Center across from Kemper Arena. How many different railroad lines and animal species can you spot here? (If you made the Amtrak trip, which list is longer?) Be sure to look at all of the photographs and exhibits. What animal is immortalized in sculpture outside of the museum in cutouts? How many different breeds of cattle can you find inside the museum and the arena? Consider visiting when the American Royal is going on. Check *The Kansas City Star* for a schedule of events and ticket information.

■ **Visit the New York Life Building at 20 W. Ninth St.** Go east and you will be walking along one of the steepest routes of the streetcars! Go inside the lobby and see whether you can find out any information about when it was built and how many different names it has had. What kind of office is on the first floor? What has been done to it since it was built? Then drive through the Quality Hill area. Which buildings do you think are the oldest?

CHAPTER FOUR

1894~1914

Making life better

If you could plan the ideal city, how would it look? What kinds of features do you think a city must have to be called great?

It's 1893, and Kansas City leaders are finding themselves at a peculiar crossroads. Almost 25 years have passed since the opening of the Hannibal Bridge. The city's population has more than tripled, and the city sprawls over nearly 20 square miles of land.

But all of this growth has come at a cost. Factories and steam engines belch smoke into the air, and the stockyards have a stench all their own. Few streets in Kansas City are paved, and most of them turn to rivers of mud after a heavy rain. Even the sidewalks are nothing more than wooden planks set on top of bare dirt.

Neighborhoods are crowded. Ramshackle buildings perch close to the street. There aren't any automobiles, so most people have to walk to work and live close to their jobs. The streets belong to horse-drawn trucks and carriages, and to streetcars, some drawn by mules. These animals leave a foul mess.

On Kansas City's rough hillsides, many of the city's poor crowd into shanties, tentlike buildings thrown together from scraps of wood. Most of the city has no electricity, running water or plumbing. The city has no parks, so children have only the streets in which to play.

To put it bluntly, Kansas City isn't a very attractive city. In many places it is an ugly, smelly, gritty mess — not the kind of place that boosters had in mind when they promoted KC as the Garden Spot of the West.

In the 20 years to come, Kansas Citians will take on the challenge of civilizing their rough frontier town. By building parks they will provide spaces for children to play and a place for nature in the city. By connecting the city's neighborhoods with a system of boulevards, they will try to redirect physical growth into a community of lasting beauty.

In the process they will create the idea of the "Kansas City Spirit" — people from all walks of life working together to overcome great challenges. Their work will reshape the city's identity. Their results will form a great and lasting monument to the future.

Filthy and rich — and ready to move forward

Through the turn of the century Kansas City kept growing in population and territory. The expanding streetcar system made it easy for Kansas Citians to live miles from work or shopping. New houses were built far from the smoke, smells and occasional floods of the West Bottoms — and far from the noise and crowds of downtown. These subdivisions made life better for many Kansas Citians.

For many others, however, life was hard. Most young people never finished even the eighth grade. They headed for unskilled or semiskilled jobs. These jobs paid poorly. Conditions at work and at home for poor people were unhealthful and often dangerous. This was particularly true for black people and for recent arrivals — immigrants from foreign countries or from farms outside the city. To try to boost incomes, labor unions sprang up. Other problems were addressed by a city welfare agency.

Girls and boys both could enjoy a new sport — basketball.

In the late 1890s, Kansas City proudly opened its new Convention Hall and in 1900 won the Democratic National Convention. But only 90 days before the convention was to open, fire struck the hall. Within hours the hall was reduced to charred stone walls and twisted steel beams.

With a tremendous amount of money and labor, however, Convention Hall reopened in time for the Democratic Convention. This success was one of the earliest credited to the Kansas City Spirit. The spirit was put to

The Junction at the intersection of Ninth, Delaware and Main streets in spring 1906. To see how this area looks today, see page 55.

the test in these years. In 1903 and again in 1908, floods put much of the industrial district underwater. The city recovered from these disasters, too.

Meanwhile, the railroads using outdated Union Depot learned an important lesson. A much-needed new station would have to be built on higher ground. That led to the

opening in 1914 of Kansas City's massive new Union Station. Many people consider it the crown jewel of Kansas City's attempts to beautify itself.

The skyline in the 1890s was dominated by the Board of Trade building (far left) and the New York Life building (left center). This view looks east.

KANSAS CITY POPULATION

1860-1920

Each bar represents a 10-year census count

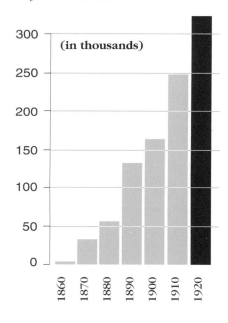

(in thousands)

More people

In this time Kansas City joined the ranks of major U.S. cities. It had grown from only a few thousand people at the end of the Civil war to more than **130,000** in 1890. In the next two decades that number would nearly double. Kansas City, Kan., was growing almost as fast. By 1910 the two cities — which contained most residents in the metropolitan area — would have a population of almost **350,000**.

Stretching the Limits

In 1897, Kansas City gobbled up **Westport**, which now became a loosely defined district inside the limits of Kansas City. In 1907, Kansas City annexed even more land. **Swope Park**, which had seemed far from town when it opened in the late 1890s, now lay within city limits. So did much of the **Blue River valley**. So, too, did everything east of the park and north of 77th Street. Forty years would pass before the city took in more land.

Passengers boarding the Wyandotte-Leavenworth streetcar line.

Getting around

In the early 1890s streetcars were changing. **Cable cars** had replaced many horse-drawn lines. Then streetcars powered by **electricity** began to replace both horse-drawn cars and cable cars. Electricity was more efficient and more reliable. Electric cars also could travel in reverse and switch themselves. By the turn of the century more than 100 miles of streetcar track carried electric streetcars. Horses and cable cars were disappearing rapidly.

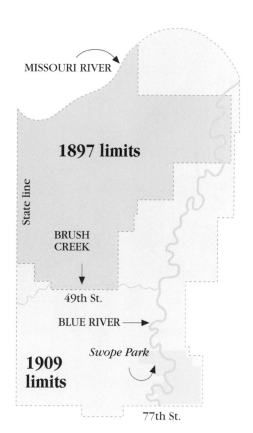

MISSOURI RIVER

1897 limits

State line

BRUSH CREEK

49th St.

BLUE RIVER

Swope Park

1909 limits

77th St.

The City Beautiful

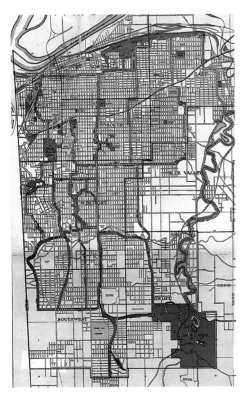

The parks system in 1913.

The West Bluffs before...

...and after the construction of West Terrace Park in the early 1900s.

In 1893, Chicago was host of a World's Fair designed like no other before it. All its main structures were built in a Greek and Roman style. There were wide avenues beside grand pools of water. These buildings and the big spaces between them gave the fair dignity, beauty and consistency.

Amid the millions of people who attended the fair were many who thought American cities could model themselves after it. This helped inspire the **City Beautiful movement,** which important Kansas City leaders wanted to join.

William Rockhill Nelson, owner of *The Kansas City Star*, thought that a prettier city would make its residents proud of it. Also, he believed, more people and new businesses would be attracted to Kansas City. He was joined by **August Meyer**, a wealthy industrialist who enjoyed nature.

Proposals to pay for **parks and boulevards** were made in the 1880s. In 1893 the first plan was drawn up and work was begun. By World War I the city boasted more than 60 miles of boulevards and almost 2,000 acres of parks. In fact, Kansas City gained one of the best parks and boulevard systems in the world.

Landscape engineer George Kessler (lower left) enjoys nature with friends. Among them was park board member Adriance Van Brunt, atop the rock.

THE BIGGEST PARK

In 1896 millionaire **Thomas H. Swope** donated more than 1,300 acres to the city for a park. **Swope Park** became the largest park in the city — and the second-largest park in the United States. Although Swope Park was far from the city limits when it opened, the limits were extended to it in 1907. An estimated 20,000 people gathered at the new park on June 25, 1896, for its dedication.

At Work

Kansas City postal workers in April 1897.

Working conditions at the turn of the century were generally less pleasant than today's. Sometimes they were dreadful.

The average American in 1890 worked **60 hours a week** and had only one day off. At one garment factory in Kansas City, workers made only about $4 or $5 a week. The average American wage was twice that.

Besides long hours and low pay, many workplaces were hazardous for employees. In the city's many meat-packing houses, sharp knives, meat cleavers and heavy tools were used to slaughter and cut livestock. Often those tools wound up injuring or killing the workers who used them. **Unions** organized to represent workers, and they began striking for better wages and working conditions.

Turn-of-the-century packinghouse workers and their products.

Manual labor was the occupation of many Kansas Citians. These men, left, are resplicing a broken cable for cable cars.

Many jobs at the turn of the century were not open to black people. Lafayette A. Tillman, left, was only the second black person hired by the Kansas City police.

The champs

By the 1890s the **Kansas City Fire Department** was considered one of the best in the world. Fire Chief George Hale trained his men well, as he did the horses that pulled fire wagons. Hale also invented many timesaving and laborsaving devices. In 1893, Hale took crews of men and horses to London, where they easily beat fire crews from other countries in speed competitions. He repeated the feat in 1900 in London and Paris. The victories not only honored the firemen and horses but also brought fame to Kansas City.

What's HOT!

A sure sign that Kansas City was getting very big very fast: Government at all levels needed bigger buildings.

The Royal

The American Royal livestock show began in a circus tent raised in the West Bottoms in 1899. At first it was called the National Hereford Cattle Show. Soon it was renamed after the British Royal livestock show. Eventually it would draw as many as 50,000 guests from out of town. The Royal, which later added parades, concerts and even a barbecue contest, become a favorite autumn Kansas City tradition.

New City Hall

In 1892 city officials moved into a brand-new City Hall. The new building at Fourth and Main streets replaced the old, two-story City Hall on the same site. The new City Hall would last until the 1930s, when it was replaced by the skyscraper city hall at 12th and Oak streets.

New courthouse

This new Jackson County Courthouse — where the county was run and trials took place — opened in 1892 at Missouri Avenue and Locust Street. It would be replaced in the 1930s by the new county courthouse at 12th Street between Oak and Locust streets.

New federal building

In 1900 this building, which housed the post office and federal courts, opened at Eighth Street and Grand Avenue. Its dome was a prominent feature of the downtown skyline. For a few years it shone bright gold. A new federal courthouse was built on the same site in the 1930s.

Convention Hall

Proudly, Kansas City opened its new Convention Hall in 1899. The famous band of John Philip Sousa played for the occasion. City leaders believed the hall would bring fame and increased business — and they were right. In early 1900 it was announced that the Democratic National Convention would take place in Convention Hall that July.

Disaster strikes

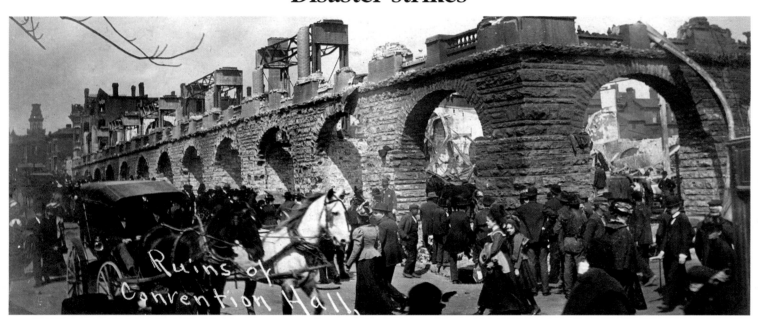

On the afternoon of April 4, 1900, **Convention Hall** went up in flames. No cause was ever found. The opening of the **Democratic National Convention** lay only 90 days away. A group of businessmen immediately began to raise money to rebuild it. Wealthy and average Kansas Citians contributed, and plans were made — this time making the hall more fire-resistant. With the cooperation of labor unions and quick work by the architect, the hall was rebuilt in time. Leaders boasted about the **Kansas City Spirit.** People around the country applauded the effort.

Celebrate!

Fifteen thousand Kansas Citians flocked to Convention Hall on Dec. 31, 1900, to say goodbye to the 19th century and hello to the 20th. The party was called the **Century Ball.** The cheapest tickets cost $10, which equaled about $200 in year 2000 money. Many participants in the ball dressed in costumes of the 18th century and performed minuets and other old-style dances. Into a steel time capsule called the **Century Box** went souvenirs and messages to be opened 100 years later.

Big doings

The 11,000 delegates to the Democratic National Convention nominated **William Jennings Bryan** of Nebraska for president. As he had before, Bryan lost. In November, Americans elected **William McKinley** and **Theodore Roosevelt** president and vice president.

Under Water

Tracks of an elevated railroad buckled near a power plant.

Heavy spring rains filled the Kansas River in late May 1903, and on May 30 it splashed over its banks. What looked like a great sea was created across the bottom land between the bluffs of Kansas City and those of Kansas City, Kan.

Services cut off

Stockyards, rail lines, packinghouses and grain elevators were swamped. Sixteen bridges across the Kansas River were swept away, including one that carried the pipe for the Kansas City water supply. For almost two weeks the city was without regular water service, natural gas, electricity and streetcars. Twenty persons died.

After the waters receded, massive levees were constructed. Nevertheless, another, lesser flood occurred in 1908. The 1903 flood helped persuade the railroads not to build their new union station in the West Bottoms.

This is how the West Bottoms looked at the height of the flooding in 1903.

At Union Depot, waters turned Union Avenue into a river.

Inside the depot, water rose within a few feet of the chandeliers.

What's HOT!

The Swope murder

When **Thomas H. Swope** died Oct. 3, 1909, his coffin was placed for public viewing at the public library. Schoolchildren passed to mourn his death. Swope, a millionaire, was remembered fondly as a civic benefactor. His most famous contribution was Swope Park.

At first his death, at age 81, was blamed on a stroke. Then police discovered that Swope's doctor, Bennett Clark Hyde, had recently ordered cyanide capsules from a drugstore. Hyde had given Swope what he called "digestive capsules" shortly before the death.

Swope's body was dug up, and traces of poison were found in him. Hyde was forced to stand trial for Swope's murder. In May 1910, Hyde was convicted, but his well-paid team of defense lawyers appealed. After the case had been in the courts seven years, Hyde was set free.

THE ZOO

See the animals!

The Kansas City Zoo opened Dec. 13, 1909, on 60 acres in Swope Park. All the zoo animals were housed in one stone building. It contained four lion cubs, three monkeys, a wildcat, a badger, a wolf, a fox, a coyote, two buffaloes, an eagle and several birds.

THRILLS AND SPILLS

Thrill riders at Carnival Park in Wyandotte County.

Amusement parks sprang up at the turn of the century and drew crowds of pleasure seekers, rich and poor alike. Thrilling rides showed how masses of people could enjoy the same thing at the same time. **Electric Park** at 46th Street and the Paseo attracted a million people in 1911.

BUILDINGS

Walls of glass

The 20th century brought new ways to build. In 1909 an innovative structure with outside walls of glass went up in downtown Kansas City. It was the **Boley Building** at 12th and Walnut streets. The weight of the building was carried by inner walls and columns. The exterior was made of metal and a "curtain of glass."

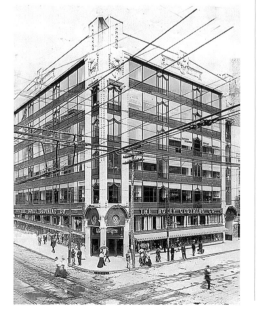

CRUSADING

Anti-liquor

Carry Nation of Kansas won national fame for entering taverns and breaking up bottles of liquor with her hatchet. On April 15, 1901, she brought her crusade to Kansas City. With a friend she toured saloons, criticizing their managers. When she gathered a crowd for a speech on the street, police asked her to break it up. She refused and was arrested. Nation was freed the next day. The judge gave her until 6 p.m. to leave town.

DEADLY CULT

Adam God

A small band of religious crusaders took on the Kansas City police on Dec. 8, 1908. The cult was led by James Sharp, who called himself "Adam God." Children of its members were begging for money. When police tried to stop the children, the crusaders objected. A riot began, ending with three cult members and two policemen dead of gunshot wounds. Adam God was sentenced to 25 years in prison.

The Crown Jewel

The opening of Union Station in 1914 guaranteed that Kansas City was now a major American metropolis. Getting the station wasn't easy.

By the late 1890s, Kansas City and the railroads that served it knew Union Depot was too small, too dirty and too inefficient for the booming city. The depot had handled about 14,000 trains the year after it opened. By 1897 it handled more than 41,000 trains. Yet for almost a decade, the railroads could not agree on where to build a new station. The 1903 flood helped them eliminate a new site in the West Bottoms.

Finally, in 1906, twelve railroads settled on a site. The new station would be placed in the bed of O.K. Creek, which ran south of downtown. Construction began in 1910. Design changes and labor problems caused delays, and it took four years for the station to open.

The architect, **Jarvis Hunt** of Chicago, planned a monumental structure that would give Kansas City one of the largest railroad stations in the United States. The new

Crowds outside Union Station on opening day, Oct. 30, 1914.

station and its surrounding buildings cost more than $10 million. The total cost was $48 million. This covered the construction of rail lines through the city. These tracks extended for miles. At many city streets, overpasses or underpasses had to be built for street traffic.

Union Station is considered by many to be Kansas City's grandest building. It opened **Oct. 30, 1914.**

Inside the station, opening day speakers hailed the grand new structure.

The Unlucky Ones

Poverty was a bleak fact of life around the turn of the century.

Poor immigrants ... and migrants

In Kansas City there were men and women without jobs, or with very poor ones. Many had come to town from the countryside, hoping to find work. Swelling their ranks were immigrants from Europe and black people from the South. The poor took rooms in cheap tenements or lived as squatters along railroad tracks. Near the packinghouses in the West Bottoms lay "the Patch," right, a community of the poor in ramshackle houses. There, a newspaper reporter for *The Kansas City Journal* found "a multitude of urchins" digging through "dumping grounds" near James Street. They were gathering discarded items, hoping to find wood for the winter or things to sell.

Schools

At the turn of the century, two-thirds of Kansas City children failed to complete the eighth grade. Often they were lured away by jobs in the packinghouses and lumberyards.

The First Pendergast

Do things for people, **Jim Pendergast** once said, "and then later on they'll do things for you."

The stories say Pendergast once bet on a horse. The horse won, and Pendergast used the money to buy a saloon in the West Bottoms. There he not only served liquor but also acted as a banker, counselor and friend to the working-class residents of his area. Like Pendergast, many of them were of Irish descent.

In 1892 they elected him to the Board of Aldermen, which governed Kansas City. Until he died in 1911, Jim Pendergast consistently got what he wanted for his district, known as the 1st Ward.

Trying to help

Some Americans at the turn of the century brimmed with optimism. One group of reformers called the Progressives thought social ills such as poverty, domestic violence and immorality could be helped by public action. Kansas City was one of the first cities to establish a **Bureau of Public Welfare**. It signaled a new idea in American government. First the board prepared a series of reports on the city's ethnic composition, housing conditions and poverty. It found severe problems in various parts of town. Severe rates of poverty and disease were found in the relatively small areas where black people were allowed to live.

Left: McClure Flats, 19th and McGee streets

Faces of the Poor

These photographs were made by a professional photographer in the early 1910s. They showed what living conditions were like for Kansas City poor people of the time. Also, they illustrated services available for the poor, such as clinics and churches.

Faces of the Poor

More Kansas City children living in poverty. These images were captured in the early 1910s.

Activities

FOR SCHOOL

Meyer

Gillham

Van Brunt

Long

■ **These streets are named for people who had influence** in the era of 1893 to 1914. Some of these people are pictured above. Write a description of one of these persons. Make sure you tell what the person was doing in this era and why he was important enough to have a street eventually named after him:
* Gillham Road
* Meyer Boulevard
* Swope Parkway
* Van Brunt Boulevard
* Strang Line Road (Johnson County)
* Longview Road
* Rockhill Road

■ **Write a note or poem** that you would leave in a Century Box on New Year's Eve for people to read 100 years later. What object representing life today would you leave inside a Century Box? Write a paragraph beginning: "For me, the Kansas City Spirit can best be described by the feeling I get when I..."

The junction in 2000. No building remains from the 1906 photograph that appears on Page 43.

WITH YOUR FAMILY

■ **Find the sites** of these places in downtown Kansas City and discover what's there today.
* Convention Hall
* McClure Flats
* The Boley Building
* West Bluffs
* West Terrace Park

look at the river below. Imagine most of the West Bottoms under water, as it was in the flood of 1903.

■ **Drive the length of the Paseo,** one of the city's grandest boulevards. What's special about it, compared with other streets?

■ **Visit West Terrace Park,** read the historical markers and

■ **Visit the restored Union Station** and look at how buildings were decorated in the 1910s. Write three questions you would like answered about the newly renovated station. Explore the new Science City space with your family and see whether you can find your answers. Return home and write a poem entitled: "Under the Clock..."

CHAPTER FIVE

1915-1939

A swinging town

Kansas Citians are entering one of the greatest periods of prosperity and cultural change in American history. The Roaring '20s will mark the arrival of many modern conveniences. People will enjoy more leisure time, and they will have extra spending money. That means plenty of public entertainments to enjoy, such as electrified amusement parks and "talking" movies.

The city is attracting an expanding and diverse population of workers and residents. In Kansas City, Kan., immigrants are arriving from European countries such as Poland, Lithuania, Croatia and Serbia. They take on backbreaking work in the meat-packing plants. Mexican immigrants settle near the railroads on Kansas City's West Side and in the Armourdale and Argentine communities of Kansas City, Kan. Thousands of African-Americans arrive from Arkansas, Louisiana and east Texas, where the Kansas City Southern Railroad is rapidly approaching the Gulf of Mexico.

Downtown, Kansas City is reaching the heights of the spectacular. Fancy hotels and bustling department stores serve local people and out-of-town visitors. Young men and boys hustle about, offering to shine shoes and sell newspapers — anything to put change in their pockets. Thousands of young women find work in the busy garment industry downtown. They sew shirts and finery that will outfit people from Minnesota to Texas. Fashion is all the rage. Simple pleasures of the future, like Wrigley chewing gum, are among the hottest fads of the day.

There's also rollicking nightlife — racy

TIME TRAVELER

burlesque shows, jazz clubs and gambling halls. These give the city a bad reputation as a "wide-open town." Young men and women come from as far as St. Joseph and Topeka to experience the city's raucous sights and sounds, much to the chagrin of their parents.

The party comes to a crashing halt in 1929. The Great Depression makes jobs scarce. Families aren't sure they'll be able to keep their homes or feed their children. The Depression is especially hard on Kansas City's growing minority populations. Many already endure terrible working and living conditions. In outlying farm towns, overplanting of crops leads to terrible dust storms. The storms darken the afternoon sun.

Kansas City persists during the Depression largely through the efforts of a notorious city boss. Thomas J. Pendergast rules the city with an iron fist. He offers jobs in local government and the construction industry in exchange for votes. The Pendergast machine backs a major initiative to build great new public buildings. Among these are a 29-story City Hall and a new Jackson County Courthouse. These magnificent skyscrapers provide jobs for thousands, and permanently reshape the city's skyline.

At the end of the 1930s, Kansas City will take on a central place in the economy of the Midwest. Its factories will churn out farm implements and new machinery that make it easier to harvest acres of wheat and corn with less manual labor. Once-distant farm towns like Olathe will be drawn into the city's expanding transportation network.

From gritty beginnings as a railroad town, Kansas City truly is becoming the metropolitan center of a vast and growing Midwest.

New gadgets and new ways to live

When 1915 began only well-to-do people in Kansas City could afford cars. No one could listen to the radio, because there was no radio. Movies had no sound and were only black-and-white. You could not get a ticket for a scheduled airliner. Only friends and family of Walt Disney knew who he was. If you were a woman, you could not vote in Missouri.

By the end of 1939 all of that had changed. Kansas City and the rest of the United States had entered an era that you would recognize today. We were in the Modern Age.

By the end of 1939 you could go for a ride with your parents in the family car — across your city and across your country. In fact, cars were beginning to drive railroads out of the business of carrying passengers.

By then you could hear movie actors talk — and see them in color. Airliners flew in all directions from Kansas City.

In these years Walt D to start a film busin

Kansas City musician Bennie Moten and his orchestra performed at Fairyland Park in 1931. Many musicians who would go on to world fame performed in Kansas City in the 1930s. Among them was William "Count" Basie, who is second from the left in the front row.

City. He failed. So he moved to Hollywood, and by 1939 you could watch Mickey Mouse, Donald Duck and Snow White at theaters all around the country.

In 1939 women could vote, and that wasn't all. In Kansas City they were aiming to lead the crusade against bad government. And were going to win. They helped remove

remnants of the political machine of Boss Tom Pendergast.

In the 1920s and 1930s, when Pendergast was the city's political "boss," many illegal forms of entertainment, such as gambling, were allowed to go on. Those same years saw the growth of one of Kansas City's beloved symbols — jazz music. As the

Pendergast machine was replaced by new, stricter reformers, many jazz musicians moved away.

The Modern Age had brought good and bad to Kansas City — all at breathtaking speed.

World War I

A great war broke out in Europe in late 1914. By 1915 most of the world's powerful countries were involved. Germany, Austria-Hungary, France and Britain fought for several years over relatively small pieces of territory. Much of the war was fought in trenches. Soldiers faced barbed wire, machine guns, tanks and sometimes poison gas. Tens of thousands of young men died, but by 1917 neither side could claim victory. In April 1917 the United States entered the conflict, which was the first to be called a World War. American troops turned the tide in favor of their allies, France and Britain. By late 1918 Germany was defeated and Austria-Hungary shattered. Britain, France and the United States had won.

Women served, too

A few women wore their country's uniform, including Kansas Citian Tiera Farrow, above. Some drove supply cars and nursed the wounded on battlefields in France. Other volunteers dispensed chocolate bars and cigarettes at the Red Cross canteen in Union Station in Kansas City.

Kansas City doughboys

Hundreds of young men who might not have seen the rest of the world went to war from Kansas City. Louis Wager stood at attention for this photo, right. Around his neck was a gas mask.

Paying the price

Some area residents never returned from the war. Musician Walter G. Shaw of Bonner Springs, Kan., left, enlisted in the U.S. Army in 1917. Overseas he played in Army bands. When not playing, he and other musicians carried the wounded on stretchers. He was temporarily blinded in a poison gas attack but recovered. In February 1918 he wrote his mother: "There is a phonograph playing behind me — a record (of) a violin and a piano. Sure makes me homesick for a minute." On Oct. 2, 1918, Shaw was killed by artillery shells near the small French town of Charpentry. His death occurred barely a month before the end of the war.

Members of the 35th Infantry Division, home from the war, paraded along Grand Avenue. This was one of many parades welcoming soldiers home.

Victory

The first World War ended **Nov. 11, 1918.** Not until spring 1919 did American troops return home in large numbers. Units from the Kansas City area arrived at Union Station and usually marched downtown to Convention Hall. The streets were jammed with onlookers welcoming the soldiers home. Many troop units marched right back to Union Station and boarded the train for Fort Riley, where they deposited their equipment and were discharged.

A memorial

When the war ended, Kansas Citians began to push for some way to honor those who had served. A citywide fund-raising drive in late 1919 raised enough money to build **Liberty Memorial**. Adults of different races and walks of life gave money. So did children, who also took information home from school.

After a competition among architects a design was selected and work begun. Hundreds of thousands of people turned out in **November 1921** to see the site dedicated across from Union Station. Several famous military leaders from the war attended.

In **1926** the Liberty Memorial was finished and opened. It was one of the largest World War I memorials in the world. President Calvin Coolidge came to Kansas City to dedicate it.

What's HOT

MOVIES

Pictures talk!

Kansas Citians of all ages flocked to neighborhood theaters to see what they called moving pictures — **movies**. But until 1927 they couldn't hear the actors talk. The only sound was usually a piano player or a theater organist playing music that matched the mood of the picture. Sometimes an orchestra accompanied the movie. Then on Christmas Eve 1927 "The Jazz Singer," a talking picture, opened at the Globe Theater at 13th and Walnut streets. The star of the movie, a singer and actor named

The Royal Theater on Main Street in the late 1920s.

Al Jolson, opened with this line: "You ain't heard nothin' yet, folks." By the end of the 1920s most movie advertising boasted of being "all-talking!" Soon theaters dropped that phrase. *All* movies became "talkies."

Get there by automobile

CARS

By 1915 **cars** were becoming common in Kansas City. Making them on assembly lines reduced their cost, so now average people could afford them, too. Across the country the number of autos purchased or owned quadrupled in the 1920s. Now it was easier for people to live and shop farther from downtown. The **Country Club Plaza** and surrounding neighborhoods could rise on land that once was the fringe of the city. The car and the paved roads built to carry it enabled the city to sprawl farther and farther from downtown.

These people are dressed for motoring in their Halladay brand roadster.

Looking chic

BEAUTY

In the 1920s beauty became big business. There were 26 **beauty parlors** in Kansas City in 1923. Only three years later the number of beauty parlors had grown to 223. People were growing more concerned about their appearance. Besides driving the right car, playing the right board games and belonging to the right church, many Kansas Citians thought it was important to look their best. **Advertising** served this need by offering cosmetics and foods that were claimed to enhance beauty.

From an ad for Creme Oil Soap

MUSIC

A swinging town

Jazz wasn't invented in Kansas City, but it thrived here for a while. In the 1920s, Kansas City was in the middle of a Midwest network of towns where touring bands played jazz and other kinds of music for dances. When the economy declined in the 1930s, bands reduced their tours. Many musical groups kept to larger cities, and Kansas City was one of the best for them. Here corrupt government officials allowed illegal activities like gambling to go on — as long as the gambling operators cooperated. Jazz often was the music played at nightclubs and gambling joints, so musicians could find plenty of work. Great jazz artists like **Count Basie** and **Charlie Parker** developed their skill in Kansas City before moving to New York.

Band at the Spinning Wheel, 12th Street and Troost Avenue.

Look at me!

Amazing feats calculated to grab attention were a feature of life in the 1920s and 1930s. **Flagpole-sitting** was one of them. A person would climb to a tiny platform atop a flagpole and sit there — sometimes for days. Usually the flagpole-sitter was paid by an advertiser. Crowds drawn to the scene would also notice advertisements posted nearby. In February 1927 a flagpole-sitter named Alvin "Shipwreck" Kelly performed atop a flagpole at the Westgate Hotel, Ninth and Main streets. He claimed to have stayed there 146 hours.

Left, crowds watched "Shipwreck" Kelly

Lots of students

School enrollments surged in the 1920s. The number of Kansas City high school students doubled in the decade. New elementary and high schools sprang up across the metropolitan area. Many of these schools, usually built of brick and stone, still were in use at the end of the 20th century. In Kansas City, Kan., the Mark Twain school, below, is one of them. The Clara Barton school, above, was built as a segregated school for Mexican-American children. It has been demolished.

Electric Park at 46th Street and the Paseo.

Fun at amusement parks

Fairyland amusement park opened in 1923. With **Electric Park** and others, these parks aimed to give Kansas Citians thrills with roller coasters and other rides. Fairyland also featured a place to keep cool in summer — its large Crystal Pool.

Enjoying the pool in July 1926 at Fairyland Park, 75th Street and Prospect Avenue.

This girl ran in a race on field day at the Country Day School in 1921.

Boom Times

The Strang Land Co. in Johnson County combined a real estate office with a depot for its Strang Line streetcars. These were aimed at drawing city dwellers to the Johnson County countryside.

The economy was strong in the 1920s. People made more money than ever. They could buy things such as electric refrigerators, washing machines, vacuum cleaners and radios. Money spent on these things went to the people who made them. Then the people who made them could spend money on other things. They could go from renting an apartment to buying a home. They could go from riding the streetcar to buying an automobile. The healthy economy brought new construction. Skyscrapers like the Kansas City Power & Light building rose downtown. The boom also brought the 1928 Republican National Convention.

New suburbs

More people with more money created a bigger "middle class." Builders hurried to meet one of the big dreams of the middle class — homeownership. On East 59th Street and East 61st Terrace, a developer promised, "a small initial payment" and $50 a month could buy a bungalow — a small house.

Nichols

Much new middle-class housing was built south of the **Country Club Plaza**. The best-known real estate developer of that area was **J.C. Nichols**. He gained a national reputation for his company and for Kansas City. His neighborhoods were considered well-planned and attractive.

Nichols neighborhoods often had curving, tree-lined streets and small parks.

The Country Club Plaza itself was developed by Nichols in a Spanish style. Nichols also planned smaller neighborhood shopping districts to serve his subdivisions. An example was the **Brookside** area, where several subdivisions were served by the Brookside Shops.

Discrimination

Many beautiful new neighborhoods built in the 1920s banned certain people from purchasing homes. Developers thought this would keep the value of property high. Often the rules — called **deed restrictions** or covenants — prohibited black people from buying homes in white neighborhoods. The black population of Kansas City increased by one-third from 1910 to 1920 and by one-fourth from 1920 to 1930. In the future this increase would mean that black neighborhoods expanded into formerly white-owned areas. Within a few decades deed restrictions would be declared unlawful.

Walt Disney

Walt Disney spent much of his youth in Kansas City. In 1920 he got a job making cartoon commercials for Kansas City theaters. Borrowing a camera from his company, Disney began making animated short cartoons in the garage of his family home at 3028 Bellefontaine Ave. He formed a company called **Laugh-O-Gram** films, but it failed. In 1923, Disney left for the West Coast and world fame.

This brief film was made by Walt Disney and shown as a short filler by the three Newman movie theaters in 1921. It pokes fun at changes in fashion and changes at the Kansas City Police Department.

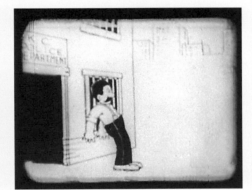

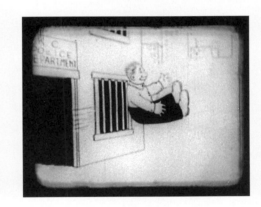

Music! Sound! Broadcasts!

The sound-recording business became a big industry in the 1910s. By 1919, 200 companies were making nearly 2 million **record players** a year. That year, for the first time, Americans spent more on phonographs and records than on musical instruments.

Only three years later **radio** came on the scene. When 1922 began, Kansas City had no regular commercial radio stations. By August it had four stations. Now Kansas Citians could listen to music that traveled through the air. Also they could hear speeches, drama, comedy and advertisements — many encouraging people to buy radios.

From a newspaper advertisement for a record store.

What's HOT

Lindbergh, right, after his arrival in Kansas City.

AVIATION

Lindy pays a visit

In May 1927, **Charles Lindbergh** became a worldwide hero by completing the first solo nonstop flight across the Atlantic. On Aug. 17 of that year he flew his **Spirit of St. Louis** to Kansas City. His visit was part of a speaking tour promoting aviation. He also helped dedicate the new municipal airport across the Missouri River from Downtown.

BASEBALL

WOMEN'S RIGHTS

Votes for women!

Although Kansas women had won the right to vote in 1912, Missouri's male voters turned down efforts to let women cast ballots in the state. Not until 1920, when the U.S. Constitution forced all states to let women vote, could Missouri women cast ballots.

Sports such as professional boxing and college football won large numbers of fans in the 1920s. Nothing, however compared with the popularity of professional baseball, called America's pastime.

Much of the credit for baseball's popularity went to Babe Ruth of the New York Yankees, whose home-run-hitting exploits were followed everywhere in the country. Kansas City in those days had so-called minor-league baseball teams. In 1923 a new stadium, Muehlebach Field, became home both to the **Kansas City Blues** and the **Kansas City Monarchs**. The Blues were a minor-league team, whose players went on to the major leagues if they were good

The Kansas City Monarchs in 1921.

enough. In the 1920s they were one of the best-attended minor league teams.

The major leagues did not allow black players at that time, so

leagues for black players were formed, One of them, the **Negro National League**, was organized in Kansas City in 1920. The Kansas City Monarchs became one of the most famous teams in the black leagues. In 1924 the Monarchs won the first Negro Leagues World Series. Most years the team was the best in black baseball.

Suffragists from throughout Missouri gathered in Jefferson City in the mid-1910s.

Hooch and a hot time

Walter Cronkite, perhaps the 20th century's most famous television news anchor, was born in St. Joseph, Mo., and spent most of his childhood in Kansas City. He grew up in a middle-class neighborhood off Swope Parkway in the 1920s. Here he recalls two local events that occurred when he was about 6 years old.

Cronkite

"(Our neighborhood was) blackened by a raid that uncovered one residence as a major bootleg operation. The house was only a couple of doors from ours, and my mother watched with horror and I with fascination as the revenuers smashed hundreds of bottles in our neighbor's driveway. The spilled whisky ran down the gutter in front of our house, and the heady aroma was enough to make the dogs giddy....

"Our hill overlooked, a half-dozen blocks away, Electric Park....One night after closing it burned in a spectacular fire. The Ferris wheel seemed to turn as the flames climbed up its sides. The grease caught fire on the two parallel tracks of the Greyhound Racer roller coaster, and twin

blazes raced up and down with the speed of the cars that once followed the tortuous circuit....

"For a child the scene was as horrible as it was spellbinding, and it left me with a lifelong fear of fire. I never check in to a hotel room without counting the doors to the exit."

— *From* A Reporter's Life, *by Walter Cronkite, 1996.*

A PARK FIRE THRILLS

Many Thousands Watch as Electric's Timbers Crackle and Fall.

SPARKS RISE AS GEYSERS

And a Shower of Blazing Embers Scatters the Crowd Below.

Gaudily Decked Concessions and Street Car Shelter Prey to the Conflagration.

THE KANSAS CITY TIMES, WEDNESDAY,

A GLOWING FURNACE SEEN AFAR—THAT WAS ELECTRIC PARK LAST NIGHT.

LOOKING ALONG THE SOUTH ROTUNDA

CROWD "SWARMS" A FILLING STATION

The finer things: New institutions of art and learning

For years some civic leaders had tried to make Kansas City a better place by improving its cultural life. William Rockhill Nelson, publisher of *The Kansas City Star*, was one of those leaders. After Nelson died in 1915, his will provided millions of dollars for a new art collection. With the help of money from the estates of Nelson's relatives and a smaller amount from a Kansas

Citian named Mary McAfee Atkins, the **Nelson Gallery of Art and Atkins Museum** was built. It opened in 1933 on land where Nelson's mansion, Oak Hall, had stood.

Not far away the **University of Kansas City** was opened the same year. It began as a small liberal-arts institution. In the 1960s it came under the wing of the

University of Missouri system, and now it is called the **University of Missouri-Kansas City**.

Another cultural improvement made that same year was the founding of the **Kansas City Philharmonic Orchestra**, which played largely classical music. Many years later the Philharmonic was replaced by the Kansas City Symphony.

Nelson Gallery

Pendergast's "Machine"

In the 1920s and the 1930s, **Thomas J. Pendergast** was the most powerful man in Kansas City. Not once in that time did he hold elected office.

He had spent a brief time in the 1910s on the city Board of Aldermen, which then governed Kansas City. At that time he represented a district based in the West Bottoms. Pendergast's older brother, Jim, had been the alderman there until he died. Jim Pendergast had run a powerful political organization in that area, meaning that he had enough friends and allies — and enough people who feared him — to win any election.

Thomas Pendergast soon realized that power and wealth were better cultivated in business than in public office. So he left office in 1915 and turned to selling liquor, operating a hotel and a racetrack, and running a concrete company. Yet his power over government continued to grow.

Pendergast was personally persuasive, making him a skilled political operator. He found jobs for thousands of people. He provided homeless people food baskets, holiday dinners and help when they were arrested or ticketed by police. All those who won his favor were expected to

You can still see the former Pendergast headquarters at 1908 Main St.

repay Pendergast with their votes for his candidates.

He also used force. His organization ensured that thugs were present to intimidate voters and overseers on most election days.

In 1925 a new plan for city government — called a charter — was passed. It established a **city manager** who would be chosen by an elected **City Council**. Pendergast allies won a majority of supporters on the council, and they named a city manager that Pendergast dictated. His power over Kansas City government was then complete and would last until the end of the next decade.

Thomas Pendergast talking in 1932 with Lloyd C. Stark, who wanted the boss to support him for governor of Missouri.

A Wide Open Town

Prohibition

From 1920 to 1933 the sale of alcoholic beverages was prohibited in the United States. Reformers hoped that less drinking would reduce spouse abuse and the number of broken families.

Illegal operations, however, kept the liquor flowing. Some were run by large organized-crime families. Others operated out of their homes. In the photo below, Kansas City police showed off a still for making whiskey. They were confiscating the still.

The law was not enforced evenly in Kansas City. The alcohol operations of friends and supporters of powerful officials were often let alone. In fact, these allies could cause the police to shut down competitors.

In the 1920s and the 1930s, gambling and other unlawful forms of entertainment flourished in Kansas City. Other cities were more restrictive. In Kansas City criminals could pay corrupt police and other officials to let their operations alone. Widely publicized murders and kidnapings gave the rest of the country a poor impression of Kansas City.

Kidnappings

Michael Katz

Mary McElroy

Nell Donnelly

Several prominent Kansas Citians were kidnapped in the early 1930s, which added to Kansas City's lawless image.

Michael Katz, who helped found the Katz drugstore chain, was forced from his car on Ward Parkway in March 1930 and taken away by kidnappers. In December 1931 a wealthy dress manufacturer, **Nell Donnelly**, and her driver were kidnapped from the driveway of her home on Oak Street. **Mary McElroy**, the 25-year-old daughter of Kansas City's powerful city manager, **Henry F. McElroy**, was abducted in May 1933.

In all three cases the kidnappers demanded tens of thousands of dollars in ransom. Some of the money was paid. All the victims survived unharmed. The kidnappers of Donnelly and McElroy were captured and sent to prison.

Hard times

Getting help

Kansas City's poor fared better than those in many other cities in the Depression. The political bosses made sure of that. Food lines could be long, but food was available.

The people shown lined up below were waiting for a free meal on Thanksgiving Day 1932. They stood outside the headquarters of a political club that was run by one of Kansas City's bosses. The children in the photo at left were helped by the **City Union Mission.**

In much of the United States, the 1930s were as bleak as the 1920s had been robust. The country entered what has been called the Great Depression. Many people lost jobs and property. Others saw their incomes drop and could no longer afford to spend as freely as in the '20s. Work on some new buildings merely stopped, and the structures stood half-built for years. Drought and high temperatures across the Great Plains forced farmers to leave their land. Many things contributed to the Depression. What's for sure is that it began in earnest after the stock market fell dramatically in late 1929. That meant that the value of companies dropped. People who owned part of those companies — the stockholders — saw their investments reduced or wiped out.

A bright spot

Early in the **Great Depression,** Kansas City still had a large number of good jobs in construction. Credit for that went to the **10-Year-Plan**, a Kansas City and Jackson County program to build huge new public buildings. The plan made possible a new **City Hall,** the **Jackson County Courthouse** and **Municipal Auditorium.**

Municipal Auditorium, opened in 1935.

Finally slowing down

Kansas City's population grew significantly in every census since the Civil War. Then in the 1930s it stopped growing. The 1940 census showed **399,178** persons in Kansas City, almost 600 fewer than in 1930. By that time, fewer than 300 houses were under construction in the whole city. At the end of the decade Kansas City was doing even worse than the rest of the country. For example, Kansas City, Kan., and the entire metropolitan area had grown about 3 percent in the same period that Kansas City's population was falling. Business leaders, who had once been confident of constant growth, now suffered a sense of defeat about their city.

Murder and corruption

The Union Station massacre

Gangster violence fascinated Americans in the 1930s. One of the most brutal acts of the decade happened **June 17, 1933,** in the parking lot of Kansas City's **Union Station**. A notorious bank robber, Frank Nash, had escaped from the U.S. Penitentiary at Leavenworth and been recaptured in Arkansas. Federal and local law enforcement officials escorted Nash by train from Arkansas to Kansas City. From Union Station they intended to take Nash back to prison by automobile. But as the agents entered their autos, they saw three men approaching, carrying firearms. These men meant to free Nash. One of the agents began firing a shotgun, and Nash's rescuers fired back. In the gunfire Nash died. So did a federal agent, two Kansas City police detectives and an Oklahoma police chief.

The scene at Union Station shortly after the massacre.

Death on election day — and forgery, too

Four persons were shot down at polling places in **March 1934,** when city elections were under way. At one voting place on 24th Street, thugs barged in and killed a poll worker. On Swope Parkway a sheriff's deputy, a hardware store owner and a political "enforcer" were killed. This violence became a symbol of how Kansas City elections were conducted by threats.

Nonpersons

Two years later another problem with Kansas City elections was brought to light — "ghost voters." These were names of people who were dead or who never existed, yet were listed as registered to vote. On election day 1936 people were rounded up to go from poll to poll, signing the name of the "ghost voter" and then voting over and over for the Pendergast machine.

A Pendergast man

Harry S. Truman owed his political career to the powerful political organization of Thomas J. Pendergast. In World War I, Truman had become friends with a nephew of Pendergast. That nephew remembered Truman in 1922 when the Pendergast organization needed someone to run for the **Jackson County Court**. Although called a "court," the body administered county government. Truman, who had failed in an attempt to run a clothing store, accepted the offer and won the election. In 1934, when their first choice to run for the U.S. Senate bowed out, the Pendergasts turned to Truman again. With the machine delivering thousands of votes for its man, Truman won and headed to Washington.

The end

The Pendergast political organization always had opponents. In 1932 they began to make their protests public. **Rabbi Samuel S. Mayerberg** courageously told a Kansas City reform group, "You've turned your city over to a gang ... of crooks and racketeers because you've been asleep."

The rabbi, like the growing number of reformers he encouraged, was threatened and shot at, yet he kept fighting the machine.

The increasing local violence and corruption finally led to an investigation by federal grand juries. In 1937 and 1938, 259 Pendergast workers were convicted in court of various charges concerning election fraud.

Pendergast helped bring himself down by gambling too much on horse races. He lost too often, sometimes as much as $125,000 a day. He arranged for money to be delivered to him from a special state account and hid it from federal tax collectors. For that he pleaded **guilty** in May 1939 and was sentenced to federal prison. Without him his powerful machine began to collapse.

Immediately, Kansas City's wild atmosphere diminished, and many nightclubs shut down. Without work jazz musicians and orchestras moved to other cities.

Winter fun: These children took to their sleds near 68th Street and the Paseo about 1930.

Activities

IN SCHOOL

■ **William "Count" Basie** was one of the most important figures in American jazz music. Known as an innovative musician and bandleader, he got his start in Kansas City in these years. Listen to some of his music and describe it using three adjectives. Take these descriptive words and include them on an illustrated poster advertising a concert for the Count Basie Orchestra in 1940.

■ Because African-Americans were not allowed to play major-league baseball at this time, the **Negro National League** was formed in Kansas City in 1920. Kansas City's team, the Monarchs, was very popular and successful. The Monarchs won 10 pennants.

They had such notable players as Satchel Paige, Jackie Robinson, Wilbur "Bullet Joe" Rogan and Buck O'Neil. Research these four athletes, or find other Monarchs players, and create baseball cards for them. Use a photograph or a drawing for the front. For the back, include significant achievements, records, physical characteristics and any other statistics you can find.

■ **Liberty Memorial** was completed in 1926 as a monument to Kansas Citians who lost their lives fighting in World War I. A citywide fund-raising drive was conducted to gather enough money to build it. Today the memorial has decayed, and Kansas Citians are again providing money — this time to repair the Liberty Memorial. Design a campaign for your school that would raise money for the memorial.

■ **Thomas J. Pendergast** was a political "boss" who unofficially ran Kansas City in the 1930s. Even though some of the things he did were illegal, many people still supported him. To examine his legacy, make a chart on a piece of paper by dividing it in half, lengthwise, making two columns. On the right side list the positive contributions he made to Kansas City. On the left, list the negative ones. Compare your lists. Decide what you think Tom Pendergast's legacy should be.

WITH YOUR FAMILY

■ **Take a family trip to the Nelson-Atkins Museum of Art** on 45th Street between Rockhill Road and Oak Street. Walk around the building to see the modern sculptures on the surrounding lawns. See what your family thinks about the Shuttlecocks — how do you think your neighbors might react if you put one in your front yard? Next go inside and tour the museum. You and your family can decide what you think is the best artwork at the museum.

■ **Visit the 18th and Vine Historical District.** Begin with a trip to the Horace M. Peterson Visitors Center for a brief introduction to the area and to pick up brochures. Next, stop by the American Jazz Museum and learn more about the history of jazz. In the discovery room, listen to different types of jazz music. Discuss your favorites with your family. Also stop by the renovated Gem Theater. Look through the gallery and try to imagine what it might have looked like in the 1930s. Finally, pay a visit to the Negro Leagues Baseball Museum. Look at the artifacts with your family. Watch the videos and try to imagine a day in the life of a Negro Leagues ballplayer.

■ **Attend an event at the Liberty Memorial.** The Kansas City Blues and Jazz Festival is usually held there each summer, as is the Spirit Festival.

CHAPTER SIX

1940-1963

Wartime, peacetime

Americans pull together in World War II and emerge from it with a new sense of their importance in the world.

Young soldiers and sailors returning from the war are eager to start new lives. The federal government creates programs to help these veterans buy new homes. The American Dream becomes firmly planted in the nation's consciousness. Houses start going up in new subdivisions on the edge of cities, catering to growing young families looking for a better life.

Booming factories manufacture cars, refrigerators and televisions in abundance. For the first time thousands of Kansas Citians are able to purchase these new luxuries on credit. High-paying jobs can be found in the automobile plants in the Fairfax and the Leeds industrial districts.

Television becomes a part of people's daily routines, often replacing chit-chat with neighbors across the back fence or the front porch. The growing availability of cars lets young people scurry about the city as never before, and makes youths more difficult for their parents to control.

One new technology has a greater effect on peoples' lives than we might realize — air conditioning. For families who can afford it, air conditioning means that they no longer have to suffer the intolerable stickiness of a Kansas City July.

At the end of the 20th century, people will look at the 1950s as a happy, upbeat time. To them, life seems to have been simpler and the prospects for the future brighter.

The reality, of course, is not so simple. People in the 1950s have plenty of worries. The Cold War means that schoolchildren are drilled each week to stop, drop and cover in case of a nuclear attack.

TIME TRAVELER

Prosperity doesn't reach everyone, especially minorities, who often face hostility when they try to move outside their pre-war neighborhoods.

Rural migrants, including Mexican-Americans and poor white people, wander through the Midwest. They pause on the outskirts of Kansas City only long enough to harvest seasonal crops. Older immigrant groups, such as Italian-Americans and Jews, often face discrimination in employment. They are not allowed to join citywide social clubs, despite their economic progress.

Sociologists studying Kansas City in the 1950s find that many groups in the city view each other with suspicion and distrust. In the face of growing prosperity and dramatic new choices, many people decide to resolve that tension by leaving the city for quieter life in new suburbs. Public squares and city sidewalks often are abandoned, places once marked by the rhythm and patter of city life.

Nevertheless, common challenges will sometimes force communities to brush aside differences and work together. On Friday, July 13, 1951, a flood destroys the homes of nearly 20,000 people in Kansas City, Kan. It disables the water supply to most of the metropolitan area, and submerges the Kansas City Stockyards and the meat-packing and warehouse industries of the West Bottoms. Nearly 50,000 people are thrown out of work.

Kansas City leaders rally. With help from federal officials and the American Red Cross, they build temporary shelters to house those who have lost their homes. Construction equipment is brought from throughout the Midwest to scrape away layers of mud 3 feet thick. Workers keep long hours reopening the city's streets, clearing railroad bridges and restoring electric power.

The flood relief effort becomes another symbol of the "Kansas City Spirit," the willingness of people to join together to battle adversity.

The world goes to war. Then comes a tense peace. Prosperity brings a baby boom, suburbs and rock 'n' roll

World War II played a big part in how we lived the rest of the 20th century. The United States entered the war in 1941, and the war ended in 1945. Spending for armaments helped the economy, and the conflict brought the country out of the Great Depression. The war left the United States as the undisputed greatest military and economic power in the world. It inspired one generation and helped the next — generations that would lead the world for the rest of the 20th century.

The first was the generation that lived through the war, both by fighting overseas and by producing and conserving goods at home. World War II-era veterans, proud of their country's accomplishment and place in the world, directed business and government into the 1990s. George Bush was the last World War II veteran to be president. He was in office

Left: Assembling B-25 bombers at the North American Aviation Plant in World War II. Center: Baby Boomer Mark Birnbaum at his family's new home in Prairie Village. Right: In 1950, expressway construction was beginning to carve up downtown.

until early 1993.

The second generation contained the daughters and sons of the World War II generation. After the war the U.S. government helped returning soldiers get an education and buy homes, creating an optimism that encouraged growth of families. This brought about the baby boom, the biggest generation in U.S. history.

The early years of many baby boomers were spent in growing suburbs, although the poor and the minorities fared worse. Most baby boomers, however, had access to television. This gave them a view of the

world unlike that of any previous generation.

Times were largely peaceful and prosperous from the late '40s through the early '60s. But they were also times of tension. Hanging over everyone's head was the threat of nuclear war between the United States and the Soviet Union. Black people began to demand their share of prosperity — better schools and equal opportunity in jobs and accommodations.

Kansas City found itself in the national spotlight frequently. Harry S. Truman of Independence, who had spent years working in Kansas City, became president in 1945. In

1950, Kansas City celebrated the centennial, or 100-year anniversary, of its founding. In 1955, Kansas City joined only 12 other cities that had major-league baseball, then the most-watched professional sport.

As the 1960s began the suburbs were growing far faster than either of the Kansas Citys. At the same time black people were striving to remove barriers that restricted them to certain neighborhoods and kept them out of hotels, restaurants and other public places. These pushes laid the groundwork for even bigger change in the years to come.

After Pendergast

With political boss **Thomas J. Pendergast** in federal prison, his political machine began to fall apart. A new study of Kansas City's finances found that the city was millions of dollars in debt. Supporters of reform called for a **"clean sweep"** of City Hall employees. They wanted to remove friends of Pendergast. In the front of this crusade were about 7,500 women who wore badges depicting brooms. In 1940 the "clean sweep" supporters won. They elected **John B. Gage** mayor and put into office a majority of the City Council, which named **L.P. Cookingham** city manager. After Pendergast was released from prison, he spent much of his time at the office of his concrete company and away from politics. He died in 1945.

Pendergast in federal court

World War II

Germany invaded Poland in September 1939. That caused Great Britain and France to enter the war on Poland's side. A second World War was under way, barely 20 years since the end of the first World War. In Asia, Japan was conquering countries. At first many Americans wanted their country to stay neutral. Those feelings began to fade after Germany captured Denmark, Norway and then France.

Arms factories

By August 1940 the United States was building up its armed forces for defense and producing weapons to help its allies. In fall 1940 the Remington Arms Co. announced that it would build a plant east of Independence to make ammunition. This would be called the **Lake City Ordnance Plant.** Another weapons plant was built in rural Johnson County, the **Sunflower Ordnance Plant. North American Aviation** picked the Fairfax area in Wyandotte County for a plant to make bombers. These factories and others would bring thousands of jobs and thousands of new residents to Kansas City.

Pearl Harbor

Sunday afternoon, **Dec. 7, 1941**, Kansas Citians learned by radio that Japanese warplanes had bombed **Pearl Harbor** in Hawaii. The United States declared war against Japan and its allies, Germany and Italy — the Axis. The United States entered the war on the side of Great Britain, France and China — the Allies.

Volunteers

Kansas City established a **Department of Civilian Defense,** which helped plan for any attack by foreign countries. Civilian Defense volunteers were trained to carry stretchers, put out fires and wear gas masks. Others helped direct traffic after many policemen were called to military duty. Hundreds of women volunteered to dine and dance with servicemen.

War factories

Now that the United States was in the war, factories turned to making products to support the war effort. **The Darby Corp.** made landing craft in Kansas City, Kan., and launched them into the Kansas River. **Cook Paint & Varnish Co.** made a special paint to camouflage Army vehicles. A large aircraft-engine plant sprang up at Bannister Road and Troost Avenue. This was the **Pratt & Whitney Aircraft Co.** It employed as many as 24,000 people, many of whom had only recently been homemakers, farmhands, salesmen or musicians. The plant covered millions of square feet, and couriers used tricycles to carry items from place to place.

Going off to fight

Immediately after Pearl Harbor, scores of young men began enlisting in the armed services. Others were drafted to fight in Africa, Europe or the Pacific Ocean. Some were killed in combat and never returned.

Teeming with uniforms

Soldiers and sailors were a common sight in Kansas City during World War II. Thousands boarded, left or changed trains in Union Station. As many as 200 trains a day came or went from the station. Many soldiers underwent technical training here in such fields as radio and electronics. By late 1943 about 10,000 members of the armed services were ordered here to learn skills important to

Soldiers sing along with a pianist in 1943 at the Service Men's Club near Union Station.

the war effort. To help all these young soldiers, many of whom were far from home, the United Service Organizations club was opened at 3200 Main Street. **The Kansas City Canteen** operated at 1012 McGee St., and the **Service Men's Club** was established near Union Station. These agencies provided such things as food, entertainment and lodging. Local women volunteered to attend dances and sing-alongs with the soldiers.

Women and minorities in the workplace

Before World War II most manufacturing jobs went to men, and the better jobs usually to white men. But when so many men joined the armed forces, women took their places on assembly lines. By spring 1944 the work force at Pratt & Whitney Aircraft was about 40 percent female. The government stepped in to encourage the company to recruit more black workers, too. This opened up some opportunities for minorities, although some companies remained reluctant.

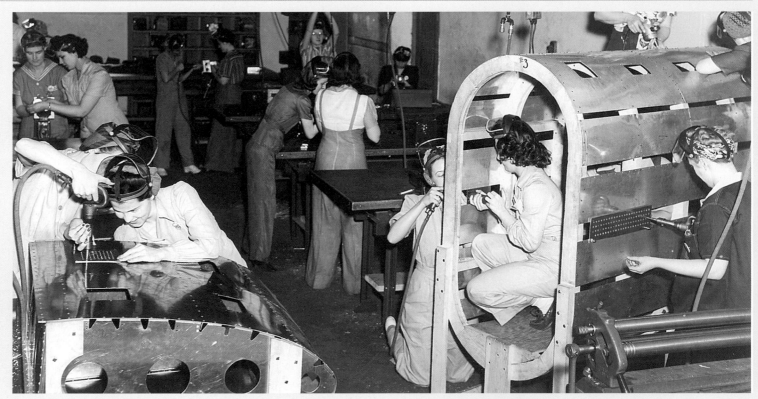

Trainees learned to rivet at the North American Aviation Plant in Wyandotte County.

Rationing

The U.S. government limited, or rationed, the use of certain products. Beginning nationwide in December 1942, rationing conserved food products, fuel, rubber and other things considered vital for the war effort. Homemakers were encouraged to can their own fruits and vegetables and to stay within limits on the purchase of groceries. Motorists were supposed to conserve gasoline and tires. By the end of the war drivers could get no more than 2 gallons of gasoline a week. Doctors, "essential" workers and a few others were exempt from the gasoline limit.

Right: Ration stamps

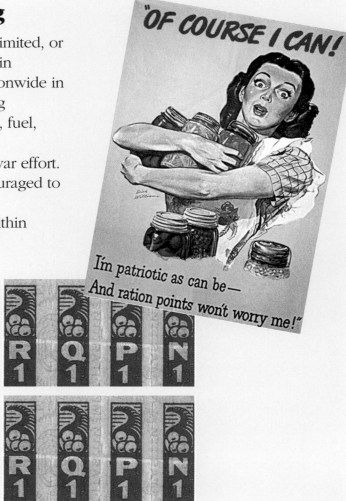

"OF COURSE I CAN!"

I'm patriotic as can be —
And ration points won't worry me!"

Scrap drives

Children could collect used metal and paper products for recycling into products to help the war effort. These scrap drives also gave children and others at home a way to feel they were helping the troops fighting overseas.

World War II

Hometown president

As a U.S. senator from Missouri, **Harry S. Truman** had made a name for himself investigating the companies that made weapons for the armed services. In 1944, **President Franklin D. Roosevelt** asked him to run for vice president on his ticket. The two won in November 1944 and were sworn in to office in January 1945. On **April 12** of that year, Roosevelt died and Truman was sworn in as president of the United States, right. Within weeks Germany surrendered, ending the war in Europe.

Blackouts

In case enemy warplanes tried to attack, Americans were trained to shut off lights and to muffle noises. Doing that would make it harder for bombers to find their targets. On Dec. 14, 1942, Kansas Citians along with residents of nine other Midwestern states practiced a blackout. At 10 p.m. they turned off all house lights, theater signs and lighted billboards. Trains were halted, and manufacturing ceased. After 20 minutes the practice blackout ended.

A big decision

Japan fought on after the German surrender. President Truman said he believed that thousands of American lives would be lost trying to defeat Japan with standard or conventional weapons. He decided to use a new weapon — the atomic bomb — on two Japanese cities. On **Aug. 6, 1945**, a U.S. bomber dropped its nuclear bomb on **Hiroshima**, Japan. Eighty thousand people died, and the city lay in ruins. On **Aug. 9** a second bomb was dropped on **Nagasaki**, Japan, and 40,000 died.

Victory

On **Aug. 14, 1945**, President Truman announced that Japan had surrendered. All across the United States people gathered to celebrate. In Kansas City thousands packed streets downtown, right. The parties lasted well into the night.

Peace Returns

Kansas City's big weapons factories shut down rapidly after the war. Other industries found new uses for the buildings and hired many of the weapons-making employees to work in them. Returning soldiers and sailors were helped by a measure enacted by Congress, the Serviceman's Readjustment Act of 1944. It was also called the **GI Bill.**

This helped provide jobs, medical care and college educations for veterans. It also helped veterans get loans for new homes, so it increased demand for new homes in the **suburbs**.

Black veterans could not buy homes in many of the new suburbs. They were, however, able to move out of the traditional boundaries of Kansas City's black neighborhood. Now the black community began extending south of 27th Street, mainly east of Troost Avenue.

Pedestrians gathered at 14th and Baltimore to watch the World Series in fall 1950. TV sets were uncommon.

Television

The Kansas City Star started the area's first commercial television station, **WDAF**, in late 1949. The first broadcast took place Sept. 29, 1949, carrying a speech by President Truman to a large banquet crowd at Municipal Auditorium. WDAF began broadcasting programs on a regular schedule Oct. 16. The first show was a live broadcast from the American Royal.

Not until 1953 did WDAF, Channel 4, have competition. That year **KMBC**, Channel 9, and **KCMO**, Channel 5, began broadcasting. A fourth channel, **KCTY**, went on the air in 1953. Many viewers, however, could not receive it because it broadcast on a different set of frequencies from the three other channels. Many TV sets were not equipped to handle these frequencies. KCTY closed in 1954.

Like radio, these early television broadcasts traveled into homes through the air. Television viewers used antennas mounted on roofs or smaller antennas inside their homes to watch these broadcasts, which in the early 1950s were all black-and-white.

Superhighways

In the late 1940s city planners were figuring out how to move a lot of cars and trucks quickly around the city. By 1949 the **Southwest Trafficway** was under construction. It was an **expressway**, with several lanes for traffic in each direction and limited access. That meant that cars could enter it and leave it in only one direction. It opened in 1950. Construction of expressways increased rapidly after the U.S. government began planning

interstate highways in 1956. With that, cities could use federal money to build these new superhighways.

In the next 20 years downtown Kansas City was to be surrounded by expressways. The result was to make it easier and faster to drive downtown and back. People could now live farther from the heart of the city. The interstates contributed to the growth of suburbs farther and farther from downtown.

Construction of the Southwest Trafficway at Southwest Boulevard and Pennsylvania Avenue in 1949.

The Wonder Years

We're growing

Kansas City's population started growing again after 1940. Wartime jobs brought thousands of new residents to the area. The postwar **baby boom** added thousands of infants to the population. The **1950** census showed **456,622** persons in the city, up from 399,178 in 1940. For every 100 residents in 1940, there were 114 in 1950. The same rate of growth occurred in Kansas City, Kan., which now had 165,318 persons. Across the metropolitan area, the population was increasing even faster. Although the suburbs did not have as many people, they were growing faster than the central cities.

A new president

President Truman decided in 1952 not to seek another term in office. The new president was **Dwight D. Eisenhower**, who became famous as a general in World War II. Eisenhower had grown up in Abilene, Kan., and still had family there. Eisenhower's brother Arthur was an official of Commerce Trust Co. in Kansas City and lived in Mission Hills, Kan. Truman and Eisenhower grew angry with one another in the 1952 campaign. Eisenhower was running as a Republican against Truman's candidate, Adlai Stevenson, a Democrat. Relations were poor between Eisenhower and Truman for years afterward.

Children from a nearby nursery visited the Centennial's Indian Village across from Municipal Auditorium.

The Centennial

Business leaders chose 1950 for a big celebration of Kansas City's first organization as a town 100 years before. This centennial was seen as a chance to promote Kansas City nationally. On June 2, Hollywood stars Robert Young and Jane Wyman performed at the Music Hall on a national radio broadcast. This was called "The Dynamic Story of Kansas City," and it was sponsored by the Hall Brothers greeting card company as the Hallmark Playhouse on CBS. The next morning, June 3, hundreds of thousands of Kansas Citians watched a Centennial Parade through the city. On June 12 an even bigger crowd watched a nighttime parade. In Swope Park, **Starlight Theatre** opened for a history pageant called "Thrills of a Century." A cast of hundreds, huge sets, ox-drawn wagons and a real steam locomotive were used to act out events in Kansas City history.

First of two centennial parades.

KC150

In 2000 the 150th birthday of the city was celebrated with concerts, big shows and scores of other events.

A Celebration of the Heart

What's HOT

TV for kids

In 1955, **Whizzo the Clown** began performing for children on KMBC, Channel 9. He was joined by other local children's entertainers — "**Torey** and Friends" and **Miss Virginia** on "Romper Room." Some of these TV personalities wore costumes, acted out comedy routines and showed cartoons and movies. Others led children in various studio activities. At the time Kansas City had only three channels. The local personalities were very popular in the area.

Frank Wiziarde as Whizzo.

Rock 'n' roll

Teen-agers got their own music in the 1950s — rock 'n' roll. It was made popular by Bill Haley and the Comets, Little Richard, Elvis Presley and scores of other singers who appeared on TV and made short-playing 45 rpm records.

Teen-agers' strong reactions to the music and to movies often surprised adults. On Feb. 1, 1957, teen-agers packed the Fairway Theater to watch "Rock, Pretty Baby!" This movie starred Sal Mineo, a rock 'n' roll singer, as a high school student starting his own band. A Johnson County sheriff's deputy was amazed: "The girls just scream, clap their hands and run up and down the aisle," he reported. "The boys throw things and push other boys and girls." One hundred twenty-five

young people were thrown out, and the projector was stopped for 20 minutes.

The suburbs skyrocket

From the 1950 census to 1960, the city of Kansas City grew only slightly. Meanwhile, Kansas City, Kan., was growing faster. But the rest of the metropolitan area grew by more than 327,000 people. For every 100 persons in the metropolitan area in 1950, there were 140 in 1960!

Touring a new shopping center at Antioch and Vivon roads.

A presidential library

Now that Harry S. Truman was a past president of the United States, it was time to establish a place to house the papers that he and his administration produced. These records are valuable for scholars. Other presidents have established similar archives, some in their hometowns. These are called presidential libraries.

The city of Independence, where Truman lived after he was president, donated parkland for a building to hold his papers. On July 6, 1957, the **Harry S. Truman Library and Museum** was dedicated by Earl Warren, chief justice of the United States.

Changing Times

Segregation

In 1954 the U.S. Supreme Court declared that separate public schools for white students and black students violated the Constitution. The Kansas City School District moved to open its schools to all races, but many white families moved out of neighborhoods in which their children might go to school with black children, so **desegregation** moved ahead slowly.

At six schools in predominantly black neighborhoods, only 117 white children showed up for the opening. Officials had expected 921 white children. Mostly black neighborhoods still had mostly

At Southeast High School, the first black student was Preston Washington.

black schools. Neighborhoods where white people were most common contained schools that were mostly white. New subdivisions often had restrictions that kept out black people and other minorities.

In one Johnson County school, black students were admitted as early as 1949. Parents of black students in north Johnson County complained that their tax dollars had helped build South Park Elementary but that their children were still forced to go to rundown Walker Elementary. A woman who lived near the school, **Esther Brown**, actively promoted a lawsuit complaining about the inequality. Parents of the black children won their case in the Kansas Supreme Court. Black students began attending South Park in 1949.

Racial change

As late as the early 1960s, Kansas City businesses that served the public, such as hotels and restaurants, could refuse to admit black people. For example, black baseball players with visiting major-league teams were banned from some downtown hotels and had to stay at hotels in Kansas City, Kan. At the time this refusal did not violate the law.

In 1960 the Kansas City Council voted to make it against the law for hotels, motels and restaurants to refuse to serve black people. Opponents challenged the measure in court. Finally in 1962 the Missouri Supreme Court upheld the city rule, called an ordinance.

In 1963 the first two black members of the City Council were elected, **Bruce Watkins** and **Earl D. Thomas**. Black people would fight for and win more rights as the 1960s unfolded.

Howard Nelson was arrested and carried away by Kansas City police when he tried to bowl at the Parkway Bowling Club on Prospect Avenue.

Troubles

Korea and the Cold War

On June 25, 1950, the army of North Korea attacked South Korea. The United Nations — which was created after World War II to try to maintain peace in the world — voted to let its members help South Korea. President Truman, who was in Independence when the North Korean attack occurred, flew back to Washington. Soon, he ordered U.S. forces to South Korea.

Many Americans feared that the **Korean War** would lead to World War III. This was one of the tensest times in what was called the **Cold War.** The Cold War put the United States and its allies on one side and the Soviet Union, China and their allies on the other.

The Soviet Union and its allies were called communist countries, after their system of government. Everyone's fears were heightened by the presence of nuclear bombs on both sides. These weapons could destroy entire cities.

Fortunately they were never used in the Cold War.

The flood of 1951

The Kansas and the Missouri rivers had flooded several times since the permanent settlement of the Kansas City area. But more damage occurred each time because more construction had taken place in low-lying areas.

In spring and early summer 1951 the Kansas River was filled to overflowing by months of rain in eastern Kansas. These rains were as much as four times the average rainfall.

On **July 13** the river poured over its dikes into the **Argentine** area of Kansas City, Kan. Then the **Fairfax** and the **Armourdale** districts of Kansas City, Kan., and the **West Bottoms** and **Southwest Boulevard** in Kansas City, Mo., were flooded. Meat-packing houses and stockyards were closed by the flood, along with the TWA overhaul base at Fairfax. Whole neighborhoods were evacuated, leaving thousands homeless. About $1 billion in damage was caused on both sides of the state line.

Above, the flooded West Bottoms in July 1951. Below, a horse is lifted off the roof where he was trapped during flooding.

Because of the flooding in the Kansas City area and at towns upstream along the Kansas River, the U.S. government built higher flood walls along the river. It also built huge reservoirs to hold water in eastern and central Kansas. In metropolitan Kansas City the speed and determination with which people rebuilt was noted nationally. **Joyce Hall**, head of Hallmark Cards, asked **Norman Rockwell** to create a painting depicting the spirit, left.

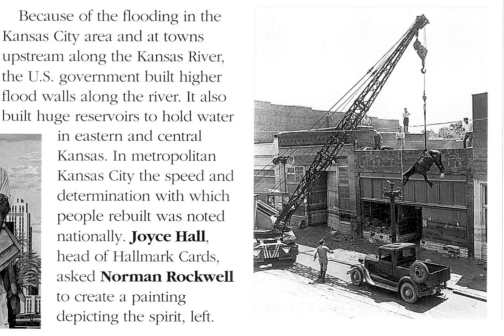

Kidnaping and murder

Bobby Greenlease, the 6-year-old son of a wealthy Cadillac dealer, was kidnapped and murdered on Sept. 28, 1953. Despite the fact that the child was already dead, his kidnappers asked for $600,000, a huge ransom. They received it in a field in rural Jackson County.

Then they drove to St. Louis, where they began spending it. After police were tipped off, they were arrested Oct. 6. The kidnappers, **Bonnie Brown Heady** and **Carl Austin Hall**, were executed in the gas chamber before the year ended.

The case gripped the attention not only of Kansas Citians but also of the entire country.

Tornado!

On May 20, 1957, a tornado touched down near Williamsburg, Kan., and stayed on the ground, tearing up buildings and farms for 71 miles. It struck Martin City, Grandview and Hickman Mills in Missouri before lifting near Blue Springs. Hardest hit was a new subdivision called **Ruskin Heights**. In the 15 minutes the tornado was on the ground, 44 persons died and 531 were injured.

The tornado tore through Martin City, south of Kansas City, destroying most of the buildings. In this view, which looks west, Holmes Road runs across the center of the scene. Right: Students help out in the cleanup at Ruskin High School.

Explosion kills six

Five firefighters and a volunteer helper died Aug. 18, 1959, while fighting a fire at a Conoco station's gasoline and kerosene tanks near the state line on Southwest Boulevard. The tanks exploded, shooting a wall of flame across the street and engulfing the firefighting crews and the volunteers. At the time it was the worst disaster in the history of the Kansas City Fire Department.

The City Evolves

The Big Leagues

Major-league baseball came to Kansas City in 1955. At that time baseball was the dominant professional sport in America. On April 12, 1955, the **Kansas City Athletics** played their first game. That made Kansas City one of only 13 U.S. cities to have major-league baseball, and the farthest one west.

The Athletics were moved from their longtime home, Philadelphia, by a Chicago businessman, **Arnold Johnson.** In the early 1950s, Johnson bought Yankee Stadium in New York. Part of the deal included the stadium used by a Yankee minor-league franchise, the Kansas City Blues.

Kansas City added a deck to the stadium, bringing its capacity to 33,000, and named it **Municipal Stadium.** The A's were popular at first, but after several unsuccessful years attendance declined.

Municipal Stadium, where they played, was torn down in the 1970s. The field is now filled with neighbors' gardens.

Municipal Stadium, packed with fans to see the Kansas City A's play the New York Yankees. It was at 22nd Street and Brooklyn Avenue.

No more streetcars

Kansas City's last streetcar made its last run on June 23, 1957. More and more Kansas Citians were driving their cars to and from work. Only a few years before, 500 green streetcars with cream-colored tops were operating around town. Tracks ran down the middle of major streets. Wires to deliver electricity were suspended overhead.

In busy times the cars ran so frequently that they were often no more than two blocks apart. With the retirement of the streetcars, only electric trolley buses and standard, self-propelled buses remained. Trolley buses were taken out of service in 1959, leaving only self-propelled buses.

CHANGING BOUNDARIES

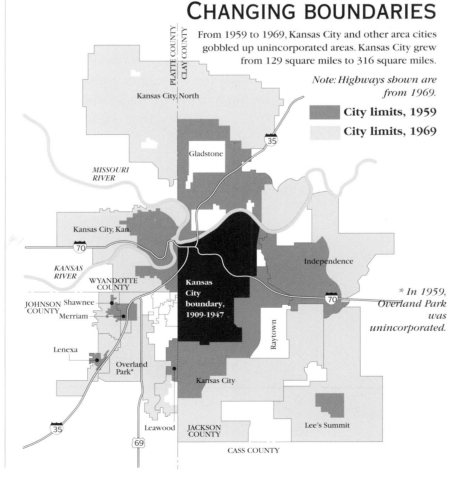

From 1959 to 1969, Kansas City and other area cities gobbled up unincorporated areas. Kansas City grew from 129 square miles to 316 square miles.

Note: Highways shown are from 1969.

City limits, 1959
City limits, 1969

PLATTE COUNTY
CLAY COUNTY
Kansas City, North
35
MISSOURI RIVER
Gladstone
Kansas City, Kan.
70
KANSAS RIVER
WYANDOTTE COUNTY
JOHNSON COUNTY Shawnee
Merriam
Kansas City boundary, 1909-1947
Independence
70
In 1959, Overland Park was unincorporated.
Lenexa
Overland Park*
Raytown
Kansas City
Leawood
JACKSON COUNTY
Lee's Summit
69
CASS COUNTY

Growing out

In the two decades after World War II, cities across the metropolitan area pushed their boundaries outward. The biggest growth occurred in Kansas City, which had covered only about 62 square miles at the beginning of the war.

In 1947, Kansas City began annexing, or adding, land south and north. These additions extended the city outside Jackson County for the first time and into Clay and Platte counties north of the Missouri River.

By 1963, Kansas City covered more than **316 square miles**. Yet, Kansas City's population grew only slightly from 1960 to 1970, when it was **507,087.** In the central city, the part that was Kansas City before annexations began in 1947, the population had declined drastically. The metropolitan area, meanwhile, grew rapidly from 1960 to 1970. It contained **1.3 million** people.

Activities

IN SCHOOL

■ The United States entered World War II in December **1941,** and Kansas Citians were ready to do their part. Many young men volunteered for the armed services, but people right here at home also contributed to the war effort. **Make a list** of the ways Kansas Citians helped out on the home front. Choose one of these and perform a 1940s radio announcement urging your classmates to help the United States and its allies win the war.

■ At one point in the war, most Kansas Citians were allowed to buy only 2 gallons of gasoline a week. If gasoline were rationed today, how do you think that would affect your family? **Interview your parents** to find out what changes they would have to make. Discuss what you would be willing to sacrifice to help the United States in wartime.

■ Official segregation of schools and businesses ended in this era. Many ordinary people worked to end segregation by protesting and sometimes even being arrested. **What are the issues you can think of** today that you feel strongly enough about to protest? What would you be willing to do for a cause you believe in?

■ Streetcars stopped running in Kansas City in 1957. This form of public transportation made it easy and affordable for Kansas Citians to get around the city. **Ask your classmates** how many of them use public transportation. Tally the results and graph them using a pie chart.

■ This chapter includes information about two natural disasters, a flood and a tornado. **Choose one of these to research.** Take your findings and make an informational flier explaining the safety precautions to prevent being harmed by a tornado or a flood.

WITH YOUR FAMILY

TV cameramen at Kansas City's first live broadcast, Sept. 29, 1949.

■ **Visit the Harry S. Truman Library and Museum** at Delaware Street and U.S. 24 in Independence. The Oval Office is re-created exactly as it was when Truman was president. What kinds of feelings do you get when you look at this room? What are some of the other interesting items you can find at the library?

■ With your family, **visit the Truman Farm Home** in Grandview, one mile west of the Blue Ridge Boulevard exit off U.S. 71. Or visit the Truman Home at 219 N. Delaware St. in Independence. What do either of these two places tell you about Harry S. Truman?

■ Kansas City had only one

The Truman farm home.

television channel, WDAF, Channel 4, from 1949 until 1953. That year KCMO, Channel 5, and KMBC, Channel 9, began broadcasting. With your family, try to **watch only those channels for one week.**

CHAPTER SEVEN

1964-1979

In the spotlight

In the mid-1960s, Kansas City begins a struggle over civil rights that will last into the next century.

Separation of people by race — called segregation — has been a practice in much of the South. That has also been true for Kansas City and other cities along the traditional North-South "border." Blacks and whites attend separate schools, live in different neighborhoods, and seldom deal with one another. A federal commission declares that America is becoming two nations — one black, one white. To protest discrimination by race, the civil rights movement begins. Young people throughout the country organize protests.

Yet despite national momentum for change, much of the problem lies in individual cities and neighborhoods.

In downtown Kansas City in the early 1960s, many businesses openly refuse to serve black customers — although they employ African-Americans as waiters, janitors, bellboys, and cooks. So Kansas City passes a new law outlawing segregation in places like restaurants and major hotels. The law is opposed by many business owners. Some of them close their doors rather than obey.

Violence breaks out when segregated places like public swimming pools are opened to African-Americans.

Kansas City's black people and white people have long lived in clearly defined boundaries. Black people have been restricted to neighborhoods east of Troost Avenue and north of 27th Street. In 1966 the Kansas City Council forbids discrimination in the sale or rental of housing. As a result Kansas City's neighborhoods are quickly transformed. White homeowners begin to leave the city, worried about the possibility of black people moving into their neighborhoods. Neighborhoods that were once majority-white quickly become majority-black.

Desegregation of Kansas City's public schools also causes "white flight." Many white residents leave the city or send their children to private schools rather than accept schools that allow black students.

Both nationally and in Kansas City, relations between whites and blacks come to a head in 1968 after the assassination of the Rev. Martin Luther King Jr. In Kansas City and other American cities, conflicts between young people and police lead to riots that last several days.

Struggles over civil rights soon are made worse by dramatic economic change.

In the mid-1960s, Armour Bros. abandons its meat-packing operation in Kansas City, Kan. The loss of the plant, a symbol of Kansas City's livestock heritage, forces hundreds of people out of work. In 1973 the Arab oil embargo will cause oil prices to skyrocket. Long lines will appear at gasoline stations. This pushes up the price of everything from bread to shoes to cars. In years to come Kansas City's automobile factories will lay off thousands of employees.

Natural disasters also will continue to afflict Kansas City. In 1977 heavy rains will cause Brush Creek to leave its banks, flooding the Country Club Plaza. Less than four months later a fire will strike the Coates House hotel, killing dozens of people. In 1979 a thunderstorm in June will dump so much rain that the roof of Kemper Arena collapses.

In turbulent times Kansas City begins a new effort to reshape its image and identity. City leaders tour the United States, speaking to officials and to news reporters in cities such as New York, Cleveland, Chicago, and Los Angeles. Kansas City, they announce, is in its Prime Time. The phrase "prime time" is ordinarily used to mean the evening hours when most people watch television. It is the prime time for advertising. Kansas City's Prime Time campaign is intended to make the same point. City leaders boast of new developments and a new spirit of progress that are making Kansas City a modern, attractive place to live.

New public buildings spring up downtown and on the city's boundaries. Kansas City builds a new international airport, new sports stadiums and a modern convention center, and a major downtown redevelopment project gets under way. Kansas City, Prime Time declares, is now a first-class city.

Above left: Inspired by the success of the civil rights push, some Kansas Citians demonstrated avidly in the 1960s. This man is calling on the government to release a Black Panther from prison. Above center: Metcalf South Shopping Center opened in 1967, joining a flood of people and businesses to the suburbs. Above right: Touring the brand new Crown Center in 1973. Right: Gerald Ford and Bob Dole accept the Republican presidential and vice presidential nominations in 1976 at Kemper Arena.

Striving for Equality

In the early 1960s many cafes, restaurants and lodging places refused to accept black people as customers.

One black man who was refused service was Richard Robinson. He owned a barber shop on Prospect Avenue. One morning in 1963, Robinson and his brother Charles walked into a cafe near their barbershop for a cup of coffee. The cafe was owned by a white man. The Robinsons were refused service. "You go into the (military) service maybe to fight for someone like that," Robinson said of the cafe owner. "You come back, and he won't serve you."

The cafe owner thought differently, saying: "A lot of my customers have said, 'If you let them come in here, we'll go someplace else.' I'll lose all of my white customers."

Instead of serving black customers, the owner closed the cafe.

The push for civil rights

Kansas City had approved a law **prohibiting discrimination by hotels and eating places** in 1960. After being challenged in court, the law was upheld by the Missouri Supreme Court in 1962. Other businesses continued to discriminate.

One of the most prominent was Fairyland Park, the city's biggest amusement park at the time. Although it had hired black entertainers to perform, it did not allow black people to use the park. In August 1963 sixteen persons both white and black entered Fairyland Park and rode a few rides before park managers called police. The 16 were arrested and jailed.

A month later the Kansas City Council voted to expand the anti-discrimination law. **The new law would prohibit discrimination at amusement parks, swimming pools, commercial golf courses and other places where people gathered.** The City Council put this proposed law to a vote of the people.

As the election drew near, business owners who would be affected campaigned hard against the measure. They said it would hurt their rights to manage their businesses. On **April 7, 1964,** almost 90,000 Kansas Citians voted. By a margin of barely 1,600 votes, the new law passed. One month later Fairyland Park opened for the season, and black people for the first time were allowed to enter.

Civil rights groups that fought or argued for these changes included the Congress of Racial Equality, the National Association for the Advancement of Colored People and Freedom Inc.

In the late 1960s, many demonstrators made their point using peaceful means. These people marched in Kansas City, Kan.

Still lagging

Despite advances, the black community was far from equal with the white community. One of Kansas City's first black City Council members, **Bruce R. Watkins**, pointed out some of the problems: much higher unemployment in the black community, and what he termed horrible living conditions and inferior schools.

Disturbances of 1968

Racial tension boiled over in Kansas City in April 1968. After the assassination of the **Rev. Martin Luther King Jr.** in Memphis, Tenn., disturbances broke out in several U.S. cities. In the Kansas City area many black students believed that school should be canceled the day of King's funeral as a sign of mourning. The Kansas City, Kan., School District agreed. In Kansas City, Kan., peaceful marches took place in memory of King.

But the Kansas City School District refused to let schools out. On **April 9, 1968**, protesting high school students marched through the East Side of Kansas City, gathering supporters. Despite the effort of **Mayor Ilus W. Davis** to calm tension, the marchers headed to Interstate 70, where they walked downtown. Traffic on the highway was blocked. The marchers went to City Hall, where speeches were made. Everything remained peaceful until someone threw a bottle and the Kansas City Police fired tear gas.

Davis

Police launched tear gas at protesters in front of city hall on April 9, 1968.

Looters ransacked a grocery at 2100 Prospect Avenue.

Incidents of random violence grew during the day. As night came, looting, rioting and burning were under way in the black community. For five nights that part of the city became a war zone. Several persons died. More than 2,000 National Guardsmen were called out to patrol the streets.

Neighborhoods

As the black community grew, black people moved into neighborhoods that had been all-white. Many of their white neighbors feared that the value of their homes and property would decline and that their neighborhood would see more crime.

Often, white homeowners hurriedly sold their homes at the first sign of a black family's arrival on the block. Dishonest real estate agents were blamed. Because these agents could make money on each home sold, they spread fear among white owners, who would panic and sell quickly at a low price. This was called "blockbusting." It led to rapid change in the racial makeup of the area east of Troost Avenue and north of Gregory Boulevard.

Fair housing

In 1967 the City Council approved a law banning **discrimination in housing** by such people as real estate agents or lenders. It was proposed by City Council member **Bruce R. Watkins.**

The measure was to have been voted on by the people April 30, 1968, and supporters were worried that it would not pass. Mayor Davis, citing the emergency caused by the rioting of April 1968, led the council to approve an even stronger ordinance. It went into effect without a public vote.

Social Change

Protests

Inspired by the successes of civil rights protesters in the 1950s and early 1960s, young people began to protest conditions they didn't like. Many young people grew their hair long, and wore beads and tie-dyed T-shirts. Among the things they fought:

■ Economic disparity and social inequality. The Black Panther party and other groups that were considered radical shocked middle-class Kansas City with demands for justice.

■ Restrictions on their conduct and course work by schools. Many objected to dress codes and to closing hours for dormitories, particularly for women. Others called for schools to offer courses in black studies and women's studies.

■ Discrimination, not only against black people, but also against women, Hispanics and Native Americans.

The Volker Fountain was the scene of many so-called counterculture events, including this wedding ceremony. Top: In 1969, UMKC women staged a sit-in to protest curfew rules at their dormitory.

■ The draft. This was a nationwide system in which men who reached 18 signed up with the government. Unless they could get an exemption, the armed services could "draft" them to fight.

■ The war in Vietnam. As the 1960s proceeded, the United States sent more and more troops and weapons to try to halt communist North Vietnam in its attempt to defeat South Vietnam.

The wrecking ball

Many city leaders and planners believed that old, unused buildings and neighborhoods ought to be torn down. They believed old structures were unusable, undesirable and often unsafe. Building owners found it difficult to rent old buildings and demolished them for other purposes.

Many buildings in downtown Kansas City were razed and often

From left: The Midland Hotel in the 1800s, as an office building, and at demolition in 1966.

were replaced by nothing more than parking lots. This gave downtown a deserted appearance and contributed to businesses'

leaving.

Typical of this was the building opened in 1888 as the **Midland Hotel.** It boasted a fancy spiral marble staircase inside. Later the building housed offices of railroads and contractors. In 1966 it was torn down and the property turned into a parking lot. The land remained that way the rest of the century.

Baseball and the Beatles

The Athletics

In 1960, **Arnold Johnson**, the man who had brought the **Athletics baseball team** to Kansas City, died of a stroke. The team was bought by a Chicago millionaire insurance man, **Charles O. Finley**.

The new owner promised great things for the team, but he kept few of his promises. For example, Finley said he would soon move his family to Kansas City. If the team did not make enough money, he said, he would turn it over to the people of Kansas City. He indicated the team would stay in Kansas City a long time. But before the end of 1961, Finley had begun looking for other cities to which he could move the team. He investigated the possibilities in Dallas, Louisville, Ky., Seattle, Milwaukee and Atlanta.

In 1967, Finley moved the team to Oakland, Calif. Finley had gone through seven team managers in those seven years in Kansas City. The A's never finished higher than seventh place in the 10-team American League. After the 1967 season, major-league baseball owners promised that Kansas City could have a new team in 1971. With pressure from U.S. **Sen. Stuart Symington** of Missouri, the franchise was awarded for 1969. The new owner would be a local man, **Ewing M. Kauffman**.

Charles O. Finley with his mule, Charlie O., the A's team mascot.

Finley and the Fab Four

At the same time that Charles O. Finley was baffling and embarrassing many Kansas Citians, he was experimenting with his baseball team. He tried various tricks to make more fans come to the ballpark. Sometimes his experiments inspired changes throughout baseball. One such change involved the green and gold uniforms he provided to his players. Before Finley, most baseball teams dressed in drab white or gray. Afterward teams began to dress more colorfully.

Other times his experiments were ignored; at one point, he installed a mechanical rabbit that popped up near home plate to deliver fresh baseballs to the umpire. At the owner's direction, one player played all nine positions in one game.

And Finley brought the **Beatles** to Kansas City. At the time the band was the hottest rock 'n' roll group in the world and was touring America. What did that have to do with baseball attendance? Finley's theory was that "today's Beatles fans" would become "tomorrow's baseball fans."

We'll never know whether his

The Beatles had a press conference at the Hotel Muehlebach. From left, they were Paul McCartney, George Harrison, John Lennon and Ringo Starr.

theory was correct. He paid the group $150,000 for a 31-minute concert at Municipal Stadium. That was the night of Sept. 17, 1964. About 20,000 were in the audience that night. Fewer than half the available seats were filled.

Prime Time

Area leaders undertook a big publicity campaign in 1972 aimed at raising the city's profile and attracting more businesses and more people — residents, tourists and conventioneers. The effort was called Prime Time. Its leaders bought television ads in other cities and persuaded newspapers around the country to write about Kansas City's benefits.

The campaign came up with a slogan for the city: "One of the few liveable cities left." The idea was to advertise Kansas City's good quality of life.

Scenes from a 30-second TV commercial for Prime Time.

Biggest of All

The U.S. economy boomed in the 1960s, and Kansas Citians laid plans for huge new structures. The landmarks were finished in the early 1970s.

Kansas City International Airport

Since the 1920s, Kansas City's main airport had been **Municipal Air Terminal**, just across the Missouri River from Downtown. Its site at the bend of the river gave it no room to grow. Yet airline passenger traffic surged in the 1960s. In addition, jet airliners were replacing propeller-driven planes and bigger jets required more space to take off and land. It was obvious that a new airport was needed.

In 1966, Kansas City voters approved **Mid-Continent International Airport**. It was to be constructed on land recently annexed by Kansas City in Platte County. The airport was renamed Kansas City International (KCI) before it opened. It was planned for motorists' convenience. Gates were split among three semicircular terminals. That made

Airline travelers in the spacious halls of KCI, 1973.

parking easy. On the other hand, the airport lay 17 miles from downtown. It opened in fall 1972.

Kemper Arena

As the Kansas City stockyards were torn down and nearby meat-packing plants closed, land became available for a new sports arena. The R. Crosby Kemper Memorial Arena, named for a prominent banker, was opened in 1974 and held the **Republican National Convention** in 1976.

In its early years Kemper Arena was home to the **Kansas City Scouts** hockey team, which lasted only two seasons, and the **Kansas City Kings** basketball team, which left town in 1985. Kemper Arena also has held college basketball tournaments, popular music concerts, American Royal events and other shows. Expanded in the 1990s, Kemper now seats more than 19,000 people.

Crown Center

Hallmark Cards Inc. led the way in the construction of Crown Center. The project sprawled across an area once known as Signboard Hill. For years the hill had contained only a few drab buildings and many billboards. Signboard Hill lay between the Liberty Memorial and Hospital Hill, named for General Hospital (later renamed Truman Medical Center) and other hospitals on it.

In the late 1960s, Hallmark wanted to create a new city within a city. Crown Center would have offices of the greeting-card company and other businesses, a hotel, scores of shops and apartments. The public areas —

In May 1973, guides showed people the features of Crown Center.

hotel and shops — opened in 1973.

Bartle Hall

The area's biggest meeting hall, Bartle Hall, opened downtown in 1976. It was named for Kansas City's mayor from 1955 to 1963, H. Roe Bartle. The hall was used for conventions, auto shows, boat shows and other displays. As years went by, conventions demanded more and more space. So the hall was expanded south over the freeway in 1994. The space for exhibits more than doubled.

Harry S. Truman Sports Complex

Hoping to bring convention visitors and more crowds to sporting events, city leaders made plans for a big new complex of structures. It would contain a domed sports stadium with movable seats, and suitable for football and baseball. The complex also would have a field house and an exhibition hall.

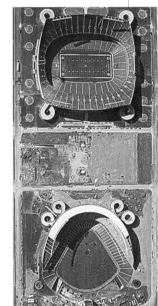

Engineers suggested two sites, one downtown just south of Municipal Auditorium and one to the east, near the boundary between Kansas City and Independence. The eastern site was chosen because of its lower cost and because traffic would be easier to handle in its wide-open space.

The complex was a project of Jackson County, not Kansas City, because Jackson County could more readily provide money. The project was approved by voters in June 1967.

By that time, the complex was meant for baseball and football only, and instead of one stadium it would contain two. The Chiefs football team played its first season in the new **Arrowhead Stadium** in 1972. In 1973 the Kansas City Royals began playing in **Royals Stadium**. In their first game, April 10, they beat the Texas Rangers, 12-1. On July 24 of the same year, the **Major League All-Star Game** was played in Royals Stadium. The National League won, 7-1.

The Chiefs

In 1960, **Lamar Hunt**, who was heir to a Texas oil fortune, helped found the **American Football League**. One of its eight teams was the Dallas Texans, owned by Hunt. After a few years in Dallas, the Texans had won a league championship but were not making money. One reason was the Dallas Cowboys of the NFL, competing for the same set of fans. So Hunt searched for a new city for his team. He settled on Kansas City. The city's aggressive mayor, **H. Roe Bartle**, led the effort to get the team.

In 1963 the team began playing in Municipal Stadium. First, Hunt had to decide on a name for the team. He considered Mules, Royals, Stars and Steers. He settled on **Chiefs**, in honor of Native American tribes that once lived in the area and in honor of Bartle. Bartle was also called "Chief" because of his work with a Boy Scout organization, the Tribe of Mic-O-Say.

Lamar Hunt in the 1960s.

Above: Municipal Stadium at the Chiefs' first sellout, Oct. 2, 1966. Right: 1968 schedule. Below: Running back Curtis McClinton.

In its first few years in Kansas City the team played poorly and had poor attendance. But the city made a big push to help the Chiefs sell season tickets in 1966. New players were added, and management was altered.

The team won the AFL championship and played in the first **Super Bowl**, in January 1967. It lost to the Green Bay Packers, 35-10. At Municipal Stadium, seating was expanded.

In 1969 attendance averaged 51,000 a game and the team wound up in **Super Bowl IV** in January 1970. The Chiefs won the game over the Minnesota Vikings, 23-7.

In the early 1970s, the Chiefs' best players began to age and their football skills declined. The Chiefs appeared in the National Football League playoffs in 1971. After that they failed to make the NFL playoffs for 15 years.

Early Chiefs players and cheerleaders.

The Royals

Muriel and Ewing Kauffman.

Ewing M. Kauffman, who grew up in Kansas City, built a multimillion-dollar business in prescription drugmaking.

His **Marion Laboratories** made him enough money to buy the new American League baseball franchise for Kansas City. He named it the **Royals**. They began play in Municipal Stadium on April 8, 1969. Quickly the Royals improved by trading players with other teams. Among these were outfielders **Amos Otis** and **Hal McRae** and shortstop **Fred Patek**. They also brought up talented young players through their own organization. The greatest of these were infielders **George Bret**t and **Frank White.**

By 1975 the Royals had come close to winning the American League Western Division. In 1976 they achieved their goal, winning the first championship of any kind by a Kansas City major-league baseball team. The Royals repeated the championship in 1977 and 1978. Each time, though, the team lost the American League championship to the New York Yankees. Nevertheless, they became the favorite team among most Kansas City sports fans.

Above: Hal McRae, left, and George Brett were key members of the Royals. Right: fans sought autographs in 1977. Below: Amos Otis, left, and Fred Patek, center, bemoaned their loss to the Yankees in the 1977 playoffs.

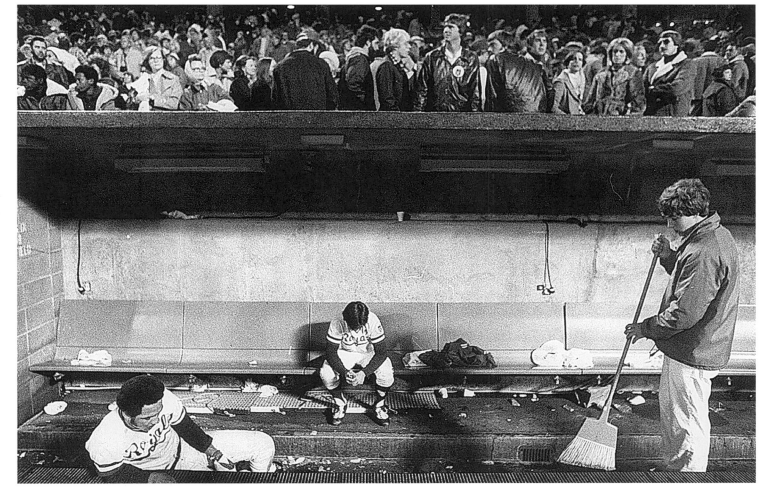

A National Convention

For the third time in its history Kansas City was host to a national political convention. The **Republican National Convention** met in Kemper Arena in **August 1976.**

   President Gerald Ford and his allies withstood a challenge by **Ronald Reagan** and won the Republican nomination. Demonstrators protesting various causes were expected for the convention. Although Kansas City police made big plans to handle these demonstrators, there was little violence.

President Ford, right, acknowledged the cheers of the Republican delegates. His wife, Betty, left, appeared with pop singer Tony Orlando. Below: Celebrations inside Kemper Arena.

Disaster!

In the late 1970s, natural and man-made disasters dampened the popular excitement generated by Prime Time, the Republican National Convention, the new buildings and the Royals.

Fire

Collapse

Kemper Arena was vacant the night of **June 4, 1979**. A violent thunderstorm raked the area with strong winds and heavy rains. The combination caused the roof of Kemper, which hung from large support beams, to fall. Various events scheduled for later that year were moved or canceled. The Kansas City Kings of the National Basketball Association had to begin their 1979-1980 season in Municipal Auditorium.

The Coates House hotel, once the grandest in Kansas City, caught fire on Jan. 28, 1978. Its south portion quickly became a mass of flames, and many of its residents were trapped. Twenty persons died in the fire, many of them as they hung out windows, pleading to be rescued. Firefighters had to battle not only the fire but also temperatures as low as 7 degrees.

Flood

Most of the famous floods of Kansas City history happened along the Kansas and the Missouri rivers. But on **Sept. 12, 1977**, an enormous amount of rain fell in a short amount of time over central Kansas City. Streams across the area overflowed.

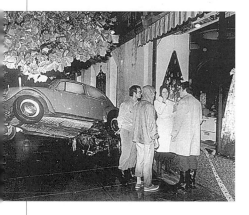

Water surged down Brush Creek and quickly flooded the **Country Club Plaza**. The flood crashed through store windows, carried automobiles away and filled parking garages with mud. Downstream, along **Brush Creek** and the **Blue River**, more businesses were flooded along with many homes. The General Motors assembly plant in Leeds shut down after water covered the floor. Twenty-five persons died in the flood, and property damage was estimated at $100 million.

Scores of automobiles were swept away by rampaging Brush Creek. This was the scene on the Country Club Plaza.

Moving out

In the 1970s, Kansas City's population declined for only the second time since the Civil War (The Depression had caused a slight drop in the 1930s). The 1980 census found about **448,000** people living inside the limits of Kansas City, a decline of one in 10 people since 1970.

In Kansas City, Kan., the population fell for the first time ever. The 1980 census totaled **172,335**.

The entire metropolitan area, however, grew to almost **1.5 million** people. Other cities were gaining residents at the expense of the two largest cities in the area.

Strike!

Kansas City faced some of the most extensive labor action of any city in the country in the late 1960s and early 1970s. In the booming U.S. economy of the times, **labor unions** wanted a bigger piece of the economic pie.

In 1969 and 1970 construction workers went on strike for months at a time. This delayed the opening of Kansas City International Airport from 1970 until 1972. Completion of Arrowhead and Royals stadiums was delayed by at least a year. At the peak of those strikes about 22,000 workers were off the job.

Even after the economy declined in the middle 1970s, various trades went on strike — Teamsters, floor layers, meat

Striking teachers at Central Junior High School in 1977.

cutters, carpenters, paint makers, electric utility workers and bakery-truck drivers.

Two unions of public employees struck in the late 1970s. Kansas City schoolteachers walked off the job in 1974 and again in

1977 for weeks at a time. Kansas City firefighters struck in 1975 and in 1979. Firefighters from other cities, other public-service workers and volunteers had to fight fires in those times.

River Quay

In spring 1972 developers opened an entertainment and shopping district around the City Market. It was called the River Quay. The word "quay" referred to the rocky landing on the Missouri River where steamboats had tied up years ago.

Old buildings were remodeled for restaurants, antique stores, art studios, craft shops and apartments. By summer 1973 thousands of people were visiting the River Quay. But a national economic recession that began late that year and efforts by organized crime to take over things in the area caused its doom.

In March 1977 an explosion leveled two buildings. The explosion was thought to have been related to a dispute between criminal factions. As quickly as it appeared, River Quay died.

Top: River Quay on a busy night in summer 1974. Left: The scene after a mob-related explosion in March 1977.

What *is* Kansas City?

By the end of the 1970s more people lived outside Kansas City and Kansas City, Kan., than lived in them. By then "Kansas City" was as much a name for the entire metropolitan region — connected by a network of interstate highways — as it was for either of the actual cities. "Kansas City" was also a media market in which advertisers sought to cover various neighborhoods in various counties. Whether they lived in Overland Park or Blue Springs, Lee's Summit or Shawnee, many people would tell others that they lived in "Kansas City."

Truman dies

Former President Harry S. Truman, who had lived in Independence since leaving the White House, died in Kansas City on Dec. 26, 1972.

Activities

■ Race relations was an important issue described in this chapter. **Ask parents, grandparents or other adults** whether they remember what they were doing when the disturbances started in Kansas City in April 1968.

■ Kemper Arena and the Harry S. Truman Sports Complex were both completed in this time. These huge structures house many of the big sporting events that take place in Kansas City. **Design a new sports arena for Kansas City.** You can create a single-sport structure or one that is able to accommodate many different activities. Start by making a list of all the things you must include; be

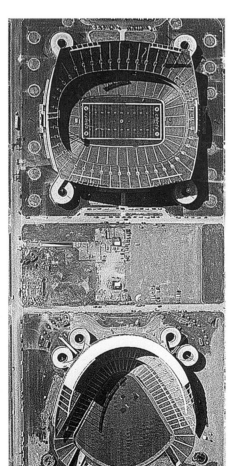

sure to make it accessible to people in wheelchairs. Are there any special features that really make your structure unique?

■ In 1963 the Chiefs played their first game in Kansas City. After a poor start they improved and played in Super Bowl I and went on to beat the Minnesota Vikings in Super Bowl IV. **Write the headlines for the Sports page** the day after the Chiefs won the Super Bowl.

■ **Make an illustrated booklet** of important Royals or Chiefs players. This is your own Hall of Fame. You must include at least two players from each decade the team has been in town. Write one or two sentences explaining why you chose that player.

■ Beginning as early as the 1950s and continuing through this era, people were moving out of the city and into the suburbs. Using this chapter and the previous one, **brainstorm a list of reasons** why people decided to leave the city.

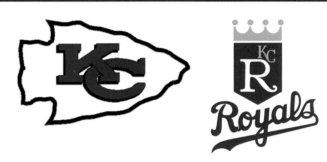

■ **Create a collage of headlines, photos, or article**s on the Royals or the Chiefs for the front of your refrigerator.

■ On your home computer, or using one at a local library, **use the Internet to look at the Black Archives of Mid-America** at www.blackarchives.org. Browse through the site and look at pictures of African-American images in Kansas City's history.

Science fair participants about 1950. From the files of the Black Archives of Mid-America.

■ **Take a driving tour of downtown Kansas City** and look at the architecture of the buildings you see. How many old buildings are left? What are some of the advantages and disadvantages of tearing down an old building and replacing it with a modern office building?

CHAPTER EIGHT

1980-2000

Where do we go from here?

In the early 1980s Kansas City finally shakes off the dreariness of previous decades. New buildings go up, changing the downtown skyline — and creating new skylines far from downtown.

New shopping malls, hotels and office buildings are setting apart Johnson County, Blue Springs, Lee's Summit and other suburbs from the city. Unfortunately, these trends are sharpening the role of the state line in dividing people from different parts of the Kansas City area.

Kansas City continues to lose population in the 1980s. A federal judge orders higher taxes to pay for school desegregation and to create an elaborate magnet school system. The nationwide AIDS epidemic and the growing use of illegal drugs threaten public health. Many Kansas City neighborhoods are ravaged by random shootings and drug-related violence. Violent crime worsens the stigma of the inner city.

After a sharp recession at the turn of the decade, the 1990s will bring prosperity for many in the metropolitan area. High-paying jobs will flourish in new industries like telecommunications. The '90s also will bring social and economic changes. Many workers will worry how long their jobs will last.

The Kansas City area still attracts families seeking good jobs and a high quality of life. More and more companies choose to move nearer the suburban homes of their employees. The economic and environmental costs of suburban sprawl will become an ever-bigger issue.

As Kansas City turns to the new millennium, great challenges will lie ahead. Downtown Kansas City was once the symbol of everything modern and up-to-date about Kansas City. At the beginning of the new century, downtown still will have a long way to go in attracting visitors and business to its once-busy streets. Despite the building boom of the 1980s, much of the central city declines as a place to work and live. Questions about race and the metropolitan identity of our region remain. These will take on a new flavor as young people question old assumptions and build new friendships with people different from themselves.

Kansas City has lived up to many of the claims made by town boosters more than 150 years ago. The area has, indeed, become a major urban and metropolitan center of the Midwest. Yet if you were to ask friends and neighbors how to describe Kansas City, you would probably get dozens of different replies.

Every city is unique. A challenge for people who live in any city is to determine for themselves what makes their city unique and interesting.

Kansas City's people, its physical environment, and its history have all been shaped by national trends. Yet like Seattle, Denver, Dallas, Portland, Ore., and Cleveland, our Kansas City has a flavor all its own. Our history sets us apart from other places. The events, the people, and the places described in this book are unique to this place we call home.

That brings us to our conclusion.

Cities are not just buildings, streets and factories. They are much more than the jobs and the social activities that take place in them.

Cities are products of our imagination. Our expectations shape how we feel about the place we live. The Kansas City of the future will be shaped, like the Kansas City of the past, by many forces. The national economy, geography, social trends, technology, and local attitudes all will determine what kind of place Kansas City will be tomorrow.

The final verdict is not up to visitors from out of town. Kansas City's image will ultimately reside in the imaginations of the people who decide to live here.

What Kansas City will become is in your hands — and in your mind.

In 1994, a helicopter installed the "Sky Stations" sculpture on top of the columns that support the expanded part of Bartle Hall.

Prosperity and Growth...

A changing downtown

After the prosperous days of the late 1960s and the early 1970s, Kansas City growth had slowed for awhile. Rising prices for oil and other forms of energy hurt the economy of the United States in the middle 1970s, and problems continued into the early 1980s.

Then the national economy began growing again, and Kansas City joined the parade. **Downtown** had seen little new construction in years, but suddenly in the mid-1980s millions of square feet were being built. A new hotel and new skyscrapers changed the skyline significantly. Among those new buildings was **One Kansas City Place**, at 42 stories Missouri's tallest office building. Much of the building boom resulted from the investments of **Frank Morgan**, a local man who stayed very private.

Despite the new structures, downtown was largely deserted as soon as office workers went

March 1987: One Kansas City Place, under construction, was on its way to being our tallest building.

home.

At the same time, new "downtowns" were being built. Large buildings and new communities sprang up on the edge of the metropolitan area. Examples of these were **Corporate Woods** and other projects along **College Boulevard** in Johnson County. People and money continued to flow out to the suburbs. Places such as Blue Springs, Lee's Summit, Overland Park and Lenexa benefited from this movement.

Plenty of work and plenty of good workers

The Kansas City area enjoyed good economic health through most of the last decades of the 20th century. Most people who wanted work could find it. And Kansas City area workers gained a reputation for good, productive work. In the 1990s one magazine found Kansas Citians took fewer sick days than workers in any other large U.S. city

did.

Most Kansas City area jobs were in services such as telecommunications or engineering. Of every 100 workers in the Kansas City area in the late 1990s, 17 were employed by **retail stores**. Because several federal agencies had regional headquarters in the Kansas City area, many jobs were

in **government**.

One in 10 jobs was in **manufacturing** — for example, making automobiles. Kansas City was the country's second-busiest railroad center and one of the top 10 trucking centers. Those plus an airliner overhaul base meant many local jobs were in **transportation**. Unchanged over the century was

the big role of **warehousing and storage** operations. Those activities were important in the Kansas City area because of its ample space and central location in the United States.

Milling, baking and trading grain were big businesses related to agriculture, as was **research** into animals and plants.

. . . But Not for All

Poverty and other inner-city ills still took a big toll in Kansas City in the 1980s and 1990s.

A terrible **heat wave** in summer 1980 led to 17 straight days when the temperature was higher than 100 degrees. Almost 200 people died. Black people died at a rate three times that of white people. The reason was that the poor could not afford air conditioning, fans or adequate medical help. Frightened elderly people in high-crime neighborhoods lived inside boarded-up houses. With no breeze or place for heat to escape, their homes became like ovens.

Meanwhile, more white residents were owning their own homes and fewer black residents were owning theirs. Kansas City

homicides pushed the city into the country's top 10 in crime rates in the late 1980s, peaking in 1993 with 153 deaths. Illegal **"drug houses"** sprang up in the city's core. Young people were recruited to sell a newly popular drug called crack cocaine.

In January 1989 a 17-year-old gang leader hired three friends to set fire to a house on Olive Street in a dispute over the drug trade. Six family members, aged 6 months to 76 years, died in the fire.

Free fans were distributed to the poor in the heat wave of summer 1980.

Schools

Learning ballet at a Kansas City magnet school.

Several suburban school districts, helped by ample tax money from businesses and residents, won praise for their schools.

But the **Kansas City School District**, still contained in the boundaries of the 1940s, was in a serious decline. The value of property in the central city, which helped determine the amount of tax money available, had not kept pace with values in the suburbs. Voters had not approved a tax increase for Kansas City schools since 1969. Among the reasons: The district contained many voters whose children were no longer in school. Also, because black children outnumbered white children in the public schools,

many believed racism played a part.

In 1986, **U.S. District Judge Russell G. Clark** ordered a plan to convert many Kansas City district schools to **"magnet" schools.** With more money and more interesting programs, the judge believed, students would be drawn back from the suburbs. To pay for the change, the judge ordered taxes increased without a vote. With the new money, dozens of decaying school buildings were replaced or renovated. New teachers were hired.

Clark

Disaster and Decay

The Hyatt collapse

The Hyatt Regency hotel was a popular new landmark on the Kansas City skyline in 1981, part of the growing Crown Center complex. Atop the Hyatt's roof was a rotating restaurant that gave diners a full view of the city. The lobby of the Hyatt featured an atrium, or open space, several stories tall. Walkways crossed it, suspended from the ceiling. They were called **skywalks**.

In summer 1981 a series of dances took place on Friday nights in the lobby. These were called tea dances. They featured traditional "big bands." On the evening of **July 17, 1981**, a happy night of dancing swiftly changed into a catastrophe.

With no warning, two of the concrete-and-steel skywalks ripped loose from their **suspension rods**. The walks fell, crushing or trapping hundreds of dancers on the lobby floor. All night long, rescue workers treated the wounded, removed wreckage and pulled out the trapped and the dead.

One hundred fourteen persons died, and scores more were injured. Throughout the metropolitan area, people were shocked. Nothing like it had happened in Kansas City — or in the history of the United States.

The collapse was caused by a change in plans for suspending the skywalks. Instead of suspending both skywalks on long rods from the roof, the change suspended the lower skywalk from the upper skywalk and the upper to the roof. This increased the stress on the beams supporting the upper skywalk. Two engineers were accused of treating the walkway design lightly and lost their certificates to practice in Missouri and Kansas. That was the closest that any official agency came to assigning blame to people.

Left: Emergency workers helped the injured out of the hotel. Above: Rescue workers examined the debris.

Union Station deteriorates

There was no better symbol of downtown problems than Union Station. By the 1980s only a few trains a day came and went from the station. Heating and caring for the old building became too expensive for its owners to bear. Briefly, **Amtrak** installed an inflated polyester dome in the lobby. Inside this were seats for waiting passengers and ticket counters.

In 1985, however, Amtrak moved out of the station into a new, small structure nearby. On March. 31, 1989, the Lobster Pot and Colony Steakhouse restaurant moved out. That was Union Station's last occupant for a decade. The mammoth station sat, deteriorating, for years.

Above: Amtrak's polyester "bubble."
Left: Few people took the train in the 1980s.

Six firefighters die

Explosions awoke people all across the metropolitan area on **Nov. 29, 1988**.

They were caused by burning truck trailers at a highway construction site in southeast Kansas City. Firefighters had been called to put out the blaze, but they had not known that the trailers contained thousands of pounds of explosive **ammonium nitrate.** When the nitrate exploded, six firefighters were killed instantly. Nine years later, five Kansas Citians were convicted in court of setting the fires in the trailers. Meanwhile, the city created a **hazardous-materials** team and a marking system to identify hazardous materials.

Floods

The water's rising!

Flooding remained a fact of life in Kansas City, even at the end of the 20th century. Recent floods, however, were not as devastating as those of 1903 and 1951.

In **1993** heavy spring rains flooded vast parts of the Midwest. In the Kansas City area, Southwest Boulevard went underwater, along with low-lying communities upstream and downstream. The levees held the rising waters in Kansas City, so the city endured nothing like what Des Moines, Iowa, and other cities faced.

On **Oct. 4, 1998**, heavy rains surprised Kansas Citians. Streams throughout the area flooded. Eleven persons died, seven while trying to cross the Prospect Avenue bridge over Brush Creek. A Chiefs game at Arrowhead Stadium was interrupted because of lightning.

Above: In summer 1993, the rivers rose but did not flood at the place where the Kansas River joined the Missouri. Below: Southwest Boulevard was flooded after heavy rains in 1993. Left: In 1998, cars were washed into Turkey Creek in Kansas City, Kan.

Growth: The Good, the Bad

The sprawling metropolitan area

Freeways and subdivisions gobbled up land in Johnson County.

Of all the suburban areas growing around Kansas City, **Johnson County** was the richest. Besides the big, new business structures that went up along Interstate 435 and College Boulevard, new subdivisions were constantly being built. Hallbrook Farms south of I-435 was as lavish as any. In 1989 a typical new home there cost more than half-a-million dollars. That was eight times the median value of a home in Kansas City. Farther west, Lenexa, Shawnee and Olathe rapidly added new businesses, apartment buildings and single-family homes.

In **Jackson County** similar booms were under way in Blue Springs and in Lee's Summit.

These growing communities surrounded a declining area composed of the central city and even some older suburbs.

Poverty, unemployment and illiteracy dominated large sections of these older areas.

Many people believed that Kansas City had sprawled too far from its core. New buildings were going up on the edges, eating up what had been farmland. In the central city, older buildings were being demolished or burning down, leaving wide-open spaces unused. Residents of the central city suspected that people in the suburbs didn't care about them. Otherwise, central city residents asked, why would they live so many miles away?

Problems in schools

Despite spending more than $1 billion on new buildings and teachers, Kansas City School District schools continued to face daunting problems in the 1990s. Children could attend a magnet school no matter where they lived. So children were sometimes bused miles to the school they had chosen. They spent hours on long bus rides, which cost the district lots of money. Judge Russell G. Clark had hoped that more white students would be drawn to the district, but it remained about two-thirds black. Three school superintendents lost their jobs, and students' test scores failed to show much improvement. By the end of the 1990s, Clark left the matter to another judge, the magnet school idea was being ended, and local control was returning to the district.

Sprint

A small central Kansas telephone company founded in 1899 had by the late 1990s grown into Sprint, one of the country's biggest telecommunications companies. The little company grew and moved to the Kansas City area, where it eventually was named United Telecommunications Inc. After laying a network of high-speed fiberoptic lines, United Telecom merged its long-distance services with Sprint, an arm of GTE Corp. By the end of the 1990s, Sprint employed nearly 15,000 people in the metropolitan area. That made Sprint the biggest employer in the area. Sprint also built a new headquarters in Johnson County. The headquarters, called a campus, was so big it would have its own ZIP code.

A plan for the future

In 1997 a "master plan" was adopted for Kansas City, Mo. The plan, called FOCUS, was the result of five years' work by 1,000 volunteer residents and city planners. It was intended to give the city a direction for the next quarter-century.

FOCUS has been described as a "to-do" list, the kind people make for things to do around the house. FOCUS aims to help Kansas City grow in successful ways. Among the FOCUS plan recommendations:

■ Build housing developments as entire neighborhoods, including stores and offices.
■ Construct light-rail or streetcar lines to connect north and south parts of the city.
■ Encourage new building near existing neighborhoods, to try to save the central city.
■ Preserve landmark buildings and historic areas.
■ Encourage development north of the Missouri River.

What's HOT

The Chiefs come back

The Kansas City **Chiefs** had few bright spots in the 1980s. Only in 1986 did they make the National Football League playoffs, and they promptly lost. In 1989 the Chiefs' owner, **Lamar Hunt,** hired **Carl Peterson** as general manager. **Marty Schottenheimer** was hired as coach. By the early 1990s the team was winning, regularly going to the playoffs and regularly selling out tickets for each game. Players like **Derrick Thomas**, **Neil Smith** and **Joe Montana** drew big crowds. On game days at **Arrowhead Stadium**, thousands of fans held "tailgate" parties.

18TH AND VINE

The good old days

A historically important part of Kansas City's black community was rebuilt in the 1990s. The area around 18th and Vine streets was where much of the famous **jazz music** of the 1920s and the 1930s had been played. Only a few blocks away had stood the stadium used by the Kansas City Monarchs of the Negro Leagues.

The **Rev. Emanuel Cleaver**, a Methodist minister and member of the City Council in the late 1980s, was a driving force behind the redevelopment, or rebuilding, of this area. By the end of the 1990s, Cleaver was mayor of Kansas City, and his 18th and Vine project now boasted the **Negro Leagues Baseball Museum**, above, and a museum of jazz. They were attractive, brand-new exhibition halls.

Champs!

The Kansas City **Royals** remained one of the best teams in baseball in the 1980s. Led by the hitting of George Brett, they won the city's first American League championship in 1980. The Royals played in the **World Series** but lost to the Philadelphia Phillies.

In 1985 the Royals were underdogs to win even their division. Then they were underdogs to win the American League championship. Then they were underdogs to win the World Series. Yet they won all three in come-from-behind, last-minute fashion. In the **World Series** they beat the St. Louis Cardinals, four games to three.

Back to Life

Through the years, several attempts were made to find a new use for **Union Station**, but none succeeded. Some even said it should be torn down. Trains were no longer heavily used by passengers, so it could no longer survive as a train station. Proposals were made to turn it into a science museum, a botanical garden, a casino and a shopping center, but none worked. As the years went by the station roof deteriorated and leaked. Big chunks of the ceiling fell out. Steel supports rusted. The owners and the city spent years in court, battling over who should fix it.

Finally, supporters of the station hit upon a plan to tax residents across the metropolitan area to save the station. This idea was first proposed by a group of active residents called Kansas City Consensus. A tax that crossed a state boundary was unheard of — in Kansas City or anywhere. But in November 1996 a **bistate sales tax** was passed in Jackson, Clay and Platte counties in Missouri and in Johnson County, Kan. Only voters in Wyandotte County turned it down.

The tax money, to which contributions were added, enabled supporters to save the station. It would become a part of **Science City**, a long-sought science museum operated by the **Kansas City Museum**. The science museum was installed in a new building just outside Union Station. The station became a grand entrance to Science City. The new complex opened in November 1999.

Fireworks marked the beginning of the year 2000 at the newly renovated Union Station.

Above: A British plasterer worked on the ceiling. Left: Science City was built just west of the old station.

Activities

IN SCHOOL

■ One photo in this chapter shows a helicopter lowering one of the **sculptures that sit atop the expanded Bartle Hall.** Reaction to these sculptures was mixed; some people thought they were interesting and exciting, while others thought they looked like alien spacecraft. What is your reaction to the sculptures? Write a letter to the editor of *The Kansas City Star* explaining your position.

■ **The growth of suburbs in Johnson and Jackson counties** made the metropolitan area much larger. Make a large classroom map of Kansas City and its surrounding suburbs. Color-code the different towns, and be sure to include a legend.

■ **Make a pictograph** illustrating the occupations of Kansas Citians mentioned in this chapter. Represent these occupations using different sizes, colors, and symbols.

■ **The Kansas City Royals** finally won the World Series in 1985. The Royals beat the St. Louis Cardinals in seven games. Write a speech that third baseman George Brett or second baseman Frank White might have given thanking the fans, and present it to your class.

■ **Visit the Bartle Hall** expansion to look at the rooftop sculptures. Design a sculpture for the rooftop of your home.

WITH YOUR FAMILY

■ **Visit the newly renovated Union Station** with your family. If possible, go through some of the exhibits in Science City. Call or write to a relative and encourage them to come visit it with you.

■ **Plan a trip to the Kansas City Zoo.** Follow the paths on the map, and make a list of each continent you visit. Also try to keep a tally of the number of different animals you see.

Ceiling in the Grand Hall of Union Station.

Now that you know all about Kansas City's history...

■ **Write a short story about an imaginary Kansas City family** that can trace its ancestry back to the earliest settlement of the city. Follow the family through several generations, ending with the story of a 12-year-old student in the year 2000.

■ **Use the glossary terms to create a set of 20 illustrated flashcards** of important events, people, or places in Kansas City's history. Take turns quizzing a partner.

■ **Create a board game tracing Kansas City's history.** Be sure to include "fate cards" of real setbacks or challenges.

■ **Choose items** you would include in a museum exhibition of Kansas City's history. Cost or availability doesn't matter. Pick the things that you think best represent what Kansas City is all about.

■ **Make up a song** that will be used in an advertising campaign encouraging people to visit Kansas City. You can use an existing tune but must make up your own words. Sing it and teach it to your classmates.

Epilogue

TIME TRAVELER

History has offered us a way of time traveling into the past. We have learned about the forces and ideas that have shaped Kansas City and how we live. We have recognized the interesting places and events that developed Kansas City's character as a large city. We have became historians who know how to use libraries, photographs, documents, and artifacts to understand how other people have lived in and understood Kansas City.

Now it is time to take off our hats, and imagine ourselves as time travelers of a different sort. Our destination is now the horizon, the future, looking forward in time with a strong sense of ourselves and where we want to go.

So, fellow time travelers, where is it that you would like to be? What do you want Kansas City to be like at the end of the 21st century? What do you, as the future leaders of your community, believe is the most important obstacle for Kansas City to confront? How will you go about tackling the social problems and challenges for the future? What do you think will have changed about life in Kansas City 100 years from now, and what will have remained the same?

There are no easy answers, of course, and the future is always harder to imagine than the past. This book offers some clues, however, and an important lesson.

Kansas City is a vast and ever-changing place, blessed with many natural resources and a striking landscape. What Kansas City becomes, however, is not up to nature. It's up to people, ordinary people like you and me, and the everyday decisions we make about the kind of place we want it to be.

Top: "Missouri No. 7" by John English

The Kansas City metropolitan area in October 1995, as photographed from the NASA space shuttle.

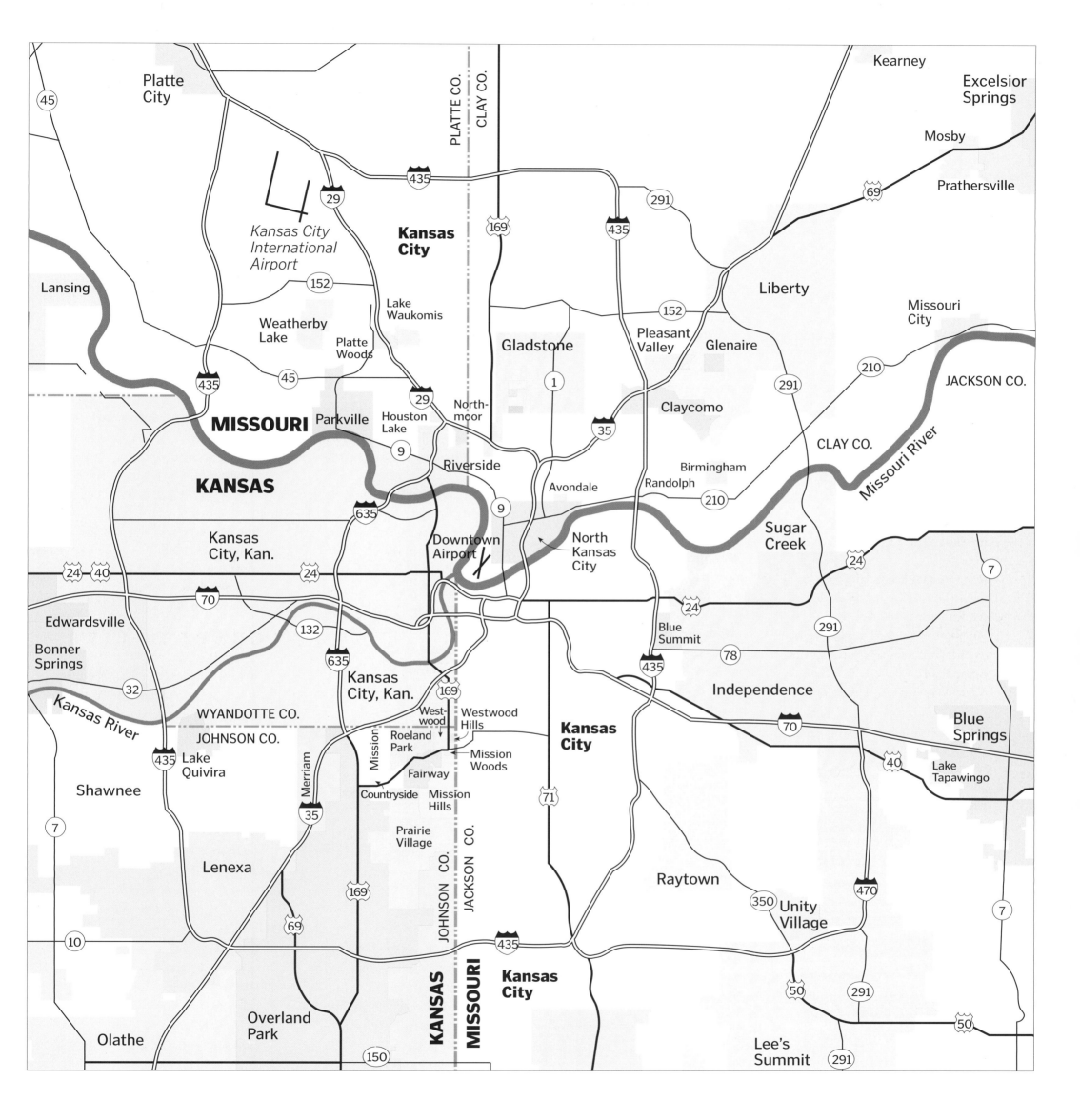

CHAPTER ONE

annex: To add territory.

bluff: Cliff or hill with a steep face.

bottoms: Lowest part of ground next to a river.

brawl: Noisy fight.

county seat: City or town where a county government sits.

editorial: Written statement of opinion, printed in a newspaper or magazine.

glacier: A mountain-like, slow-moving mass of ice.

keel: Central, front-to-back structural segment in the bottom of a boat's hull.

landing: Place where people or goods land after a trip. The place where boat travelers go ashore.

landscape: natural scenery.

mission: Place where missionaries work.

missionary: Person sent by a church to do religious work, sometimes to convert others to a religion.

Mormon: Member of the Church of Jesus Christ of Latter-day Saints.

prospector: A person who searches for valuable resources, such as gold or silver.

Quaker: A member of the Society of Friends, a Christian religious organization noted for pacifism and for opposition to slavery.

reservation: Land set apart for a special purpose.

persecute: To trouble or annoy, often because of religion or ethnic group.

sandbar: Area of sand formed by river currents.

sediment: stones, sand or other material deposited by water.

snag: Tree or branch in a river that can hamper boat travel.

surveyor: One who finds the exact dimensions of land by measurement and calculation.

tar and feather: To humiliate someone by covering him or her with tar and feathers.

tariffs: Costs charged by countries for bringing in products from other countries. Used to raise money or to discourage imports.

trustee: Person appointed to administer the affairs of an institution.

yeoman: Person who cultivates his own land.

CHAPTER TWO

Bushwhacker: Pro-slavery fighter engaged in plunder and property destruction. Also called border ruffian.

Confederate: Supporter of the Confederate States of America, the South in the Civil War.

curfew: Rule requiring a person to be home at a certain time.

free-soilers: People who did not want slavery in a territory.

garrison: A permanent military post.

guerrilla: Member of a group of warriors that is not part of a regular army.

Jayhawker: Anti-slavery fighter engaged in plunder and marauding.

partisan: Ardent supporter of a cause.

plunder: To rob by force, especially in a war.

referendum: Decision by voters on a law or a rule.

ruffian: Lawless, brutal bully.

secede: To formally leave or drop out of a group.

sympathizer: One who agrees with another's opinion.

scaffold: Raised platform.

transcontinental: Crossing a continent.

Union: Federal government of the United States in the Civil War.

CHAPTER THREE

abolitionist: Person who wants to end or abolish slavery.

bluff: Cliff or hill with a steep face.

caisson: Watertight chamber that allows work under water.

Exodusters: Former slaves and their families who moved from the South to the Midwest in the late 19th century. From the word "exodus" in the Bible, a mass departure of people.

falseworks: Temporary framework used in construction.

genesis: Origin of something.

gully: Small valley or ravine.

locale: A place.

livestock exchange: A place where cattle, hogs or other animals are bought and sold, usually open only to members.

Mennonite: Member of a Protestant religious group that favors simple living.

pier: A pillar that supports a bridge.

pivot draw: Part of a bridge that can be opened by rotating atop its pier, allowing tall boats to pass.

Priests of Pallas: Annual Kansas City celebration of the late 19th and early 20th centuries.

railhead: The farthest point to which a railroad extends.

Reconstruction: Reorganization of the formerly Confederate Southern states after the Civil War.

stockyards: Pens where cattle, sheep and hogs can be kept temporarily.

CHAPTER FOUR

alderman: Member of a city governing body, which is often called a Board of Aldermen.

American Royal: Annual Kansas City livestock and horse show.

annex: To add territory.

benefactor: One who benefits another person or group, often with a large amount of money.

boulevard: Wide city street, usually with space for grass and trees at the sides or in the center.

boosters: Energetic supporter of a thing or a cause.

Bureau of Public Welfare: Kansas City agency that studied poverty and other social issues in the 1910s.

Century Box: A box in which Kansas Citians attending the Century Ball left messages and items on Dec. 31, 1900, and Jan. 1, 1901. The box was sealed and not to be opened until Jan. 1, 2001, the beginning of the next century.

immigrant: A person who moves or migrates to another place or country.

levee: Barrier built along a stream to prevent floods.

tenement: Often overcrowded apartment house.

shanty: Crude house.

squatter: A person who occupies land without having permission or without paying.

transients: People who stay one place only a short time.

ward: District of a city.

welfare agency: Official group assigned to help the poor.

CHAPTER FIVE

allies: Countries or people that unite for some common purpose. In World Wars I and II, Great Britain and France were allies against Germany. They were joined by the United States. Also: Friends or supporters of a politician.

animated: Drawings made to move in a lifelike way.

architects: Designers of buildings.

aviation: The use of airplanes and other aircraft.

ballot: A piece of paper on which a voter marks choices. Also: A round of voting.

banned: Prohibited, not allowed.

boss: Leader and decision-maker.

burlesque: Comic stage show.

calculated: Planned or intended, thought out beforehand.

canteen: Snack bar, place of free entertainment.

confiscated: Seized or taken by

some authority.

convicted: Found guilty of a crime.

corrupt: Dishonest or immoral.

dedicated: To commit or set apart for some purpose, often with ceremony.

deed restrictions: Rules set down in contracts for the sale of houses, sometimes keeping certain people from buying them.

dispensed: Distributed, gave out.

enforcer: Someone charged with keeping others loyal or obedient.

exploits: Great deeds.

feats: Noteworthy acts or achievements.

flourished: Thrived.

fixed: Dishonestly arranged beforehand.

ghost voters: Voters using names other than their own, usually of non-existent people.

immigrant: A person who moves or migrates to another place or country.

initiative: An act leading to some result.

leisure: Time free from work or other duties.

middle class: Social group with average income, living in average homes and spending an average amount of money. Its members are neither rich nor poor, but in between.

notorious: Widely known, mostly in a bad way.

outlying: Remote, existing at a distance from something.

phonographs: Sound-making machines that played records, which were grooved discs or cylinders made of wax or plastic.

political machine: An organization that controls a political party or the government in a city or another jurisdiction.

prominent: Important or well-known.

racketeer: Person doing organized, illegal activities.

racy: Vigorous, slightly improper.

rollicking: Carefree and spirited.

quadrupled: Multiplied by four.

raucous: Rowdy or disorderly.

sprawling: Spreading or stretching out, usually in an unplanned or awkward way.

trenches: Ditches dug in the ground for protection on the battlefield.

wide-open: Tolerant of illegal or immoral activities.

C H A P T E R   S I X

annexing: Adding territory by law or force

armaments: Weapons and ammunition used for warfare.

baby boom: The large number of children born in the United States after World War II.

camouflage: Use of colors and textures to make it difficult to see an object, usually as protection against an enemy.

centennial: 100th anniversary.

Cold War: State of conflict and tension between the Soviet Union and the United States that lasted from the end of World War II until the late 1980s. Neither of the two great powers attacked the other, which would have started a "hot" war.

couriers: Message-carriers.

desegregation: End of separating people by race in schools or other places.

discrimination: Action based on prejudice or partiality.

engulfing: Swallowing up.

metropolitan: Referring to a large city and its surrounding communities.

prosperity: Good fortune, wealth.

recruit: To seek out someone for a job or role.

rationing: Limiting the amount of something that people may have.

reservoirs: Artificial lakes where water is kept to prevent floods or to relieve drought.

segregation: The separation of people by race.

sociologist: Person who studies the structure and development of relations among people.

subdivision: Land divided into lots for building.

suburbs: Communities near a large city.

surrender: To give up to the enemy in war.

veterans: Former members of the armed services

C H A P T E R   S E V E N

annex: To add territory.

assassination: Murder of a politically prominent person.

census: Official counting of the population, done every 10 years in the United States.

conventioneers: People who participate in a large meeting or a convention.

discrimination: Action based on prejudice or partiality.

dormitories: Buildings with rooms for residents, often at colleges.

embargo: To block commerce.

exemption: Being immune or free from having to do or pay something.

factions: Groups within larger groups, such as political parties.

franchise: The right to own and operate a professional sports team, granted by a league.

inequality: Differences in treatment of people.

inundated: Flooded.

labor union: Organization of workers for helping one another and for dealing with employers.

nomination: Selection or recommendation as a candidate for office.

protesting: Objecting or disapproving.

raze: To tear down a structure.

recession: Time of economic decline, when the number of jobs and the number of things produced drop.

segregation: The separation of people by race.

strike: Refusal by workers to do their jobs, aimed at winning something from management.

tourists: People who visit a place, usually on vacation.

unscrupulous: Acting without principle.

C H A P T E R   E I G H T

atrium: High, skylighted or open lobby or court.

bistate: Action agreed on or taken by two states.

collapse: To fall to the ground, cave in.

daunting: Causing fear or worry.

deteriorating: Going bad, falling apart.

epidemic: Outbreak of disease that affects many people at once.

fiberoptics: Use of fine glass tubes or wires that use light fibers to send information long distances.

hazardous: Dangerous.

levees: Embankments meant to keep water from flooding surrounding areas.

mammoth: Huge.

prosperous: Wealthy, thriving.

redevelopment: Rebuilding or replacing a building or neighborhood.

renovate: Repair to good condition.

school superintendent: Leader of a school district.

stigma: Mark of disgrace or discredit.

subdivision: Land divided into lots for building.

suburb: Community adjoining a large city.

telecommunications: The process of sending information by electromagnetic signals, as in telephones, radio or television.

BOOKS

These books are only some of the many that deal with Kansas City area history. Many are still in print, and all should be available at public libraries in the area.

GENERAL HISTORIES

A. Theodore Brown and **Lyle W. Dorsett.** *K.C.: A History of Kansas City, Missouri.* Boulder, Colo.: Pruett Publishing, 1978.

A. Theodore Brown. *Frontier Community: Kansas City to 1870.* Columbia: University of Missouri Press, 1963.

Henry C. Haskell Jr. and **Richard B. Fowler.** *City of the Future.* Kansas City: Frank Glenn Publishing, 1950.

Rick Montgomery and **Shirl Kasper, Monroe Dodd ed.** *Kansas City: An American Story.* Kansas City: Kansas City Star Books, 1999.

Sherry Lamb Schirmer and **Richard D. McKinzie.** *At the River's Bend: An Illustrated History of Kansas City, Independence & Jackson County.* Woodland Hills, Calif.: Windsor Publications Inc., in association with the Jackson County Historical Society, 1982.

ARCHITECTURE AND BUILDINGS

Dory DeAngelo and **Jane Fifield Flynn.** *Kansas City Style.* Kansas City: Harrow Books, 1990.

George Erhlich. *Kansas City, Missouri: An Architectural History, 1826-1990.* Columbia: University of Missouri Press, 1992.

BORDER CONFLICT AND CIVIL WAR

Michael Fellman. *Inside War: The guerrilla conflict in Missouri during the American Civil War.* New York: Oxford University Press, 1989.

Howard N. Monnett. *Action Before Westport, 1864.* Kansas City: Westport Historical Society, 1964. Revised edition, Niwot, Colo: University Press of Colorado, 1995.

EARLY FRENCH SETTLERS

Charles E. Hoffhaus. *Chez les Canses: Three Centuries at Kawsmouth.* Kansas City: Lowell Press, 1984.

FRONTIER TRAILS

Jami Parkison. *Path to Glory: A Pictorial Celebration of the Santa Fe Trail.* Kansas City: Highwater Editions, 1996.

PARKS AND BEAUTIFICATION

William H. Wilson. *The City Beautiful Movement in Kansas City.* Columbia: University of Missouri Press, 1989.

William H. Worley. *J.C. Nichols and the Shaping of Kansas City.* Columbia: University of Missouri Press, 1990.

RAILROADS

Charles N. Glaab. *Kansas City and the Railroads: Community Policy in the Growth of a Regional Metropolis.* Lawrence: University Press of Kansas, 1993.

Jeffrey Spivak. *Union Station: Kansas City.* Kansas City: Kansas City Star Books, 1999.

PENDERGAST

Lawrence H. Larsen and **Nancy J. Hulston.** *Pendergast!* Columbia: University of Missouri Press, 1997.

William M. Reddig. *Tom's Town: Kansas City and the Pendergast Legend.* Columbia: University of Missouri Press, 1986.

WOMEN

Jane Fifield Flynn. *Kansas City Women of Independent Minds.* Kansas City: Fifield Pub. Co., 1992.

OTHER

Carolyn Glenn Brewer. *Caught in the Path: The Ruskin Heights Tornado.* Kansas City: Prairie Fugue Books, 1997.

Janet Bruce. *The Kansas City Monarchs: Champions of Black Baseball.* Lawrence: University Press of Kansas, 1985.

David McCullough. *Truman.* New York: Simon & Schuster, 1992.

Wilda Sandy. *Here Lies Kansas City: A Collection of Our City's Notables and Their Final Resting Places.* Kansas City: Bennett-Schneider Inc., 1984.

James L. Soward. *Hospital Hill.* Kansas City: Truman Medical Center Charitable Foundation, 1995.

Robert Unger. *The Union Station Massacre.* Kansas City: Andrews McMeel Publishing, 1997.

LIBRARIES AND ARCHIVES

There are scores of libraries and archives, large and small, throughout the metropolitan area. These are some of the main ones.

Special Collections Department, Kansas City Public Library. Third floor, 311 E. 12th St., Kansas City, Mo.

Western Historical Manuscript Collection, University of Missouri-Kansas City. Newcomb Hall, Room 302, UMKC.

Central Resource Library, Johnson County Library. 9875 W. 87th St., Overland Park, Kan.

Wyandotte County Historical Society & Museum. 631 N. 126th St., Bonner Springs, Kan.

Jackson County Historical Society. Room 103, Independence Square Courthouse, 112 W. Lexington, Independence, Mo.

Kansas City, Kansas, Public Library. 625 Minnesota Ave., Kansas City, Kan.

Mid-Continent Public Library. Locations throughout the Northland and in eastern Jackson County.

Kansas State Historical Society. 6425 S.W. Sixth Ave., Topeka, Kan.

State Historical Society of Missouri. 1020 Lowry St., Columbia, Mo.

MUSEUMS

As with libraries and archives, scores of museums dot the metropolitan area, many of them small collections devoted to specialties or neighborhoods. Here are a few interesting museums.

The Ben Ferrel Platte County Museum. 222 Ferrel St., Platte City. An 1882 living history Victorian minimansion that tells the story of Platte County.

Clay County Museum & Historical Society. 14 N. Main, Liberty, Mo. 64068.

Fort Osage. Sibley in eastern Jackson County. Reconstructed former Indian trading post and military garrison.

Johnson County Museum of History, 6305 Lackman Rd., Shawnee, Kan.

Kansas City Museum. 3218 Gladstone Blvd., Kansas City, Mo. Displays of area history extending into the second half of the 19th century.

Liberty Memorial Museum of World War I. North end of Penn Valley Park, Kansas City. Closed for repairs in the late 1990s. When open, it contains a museum of World War I artifacts and a 217-foot tower with a sweeping view of Kansas City.

Missouri Town 1855. East side of Lake Jacomo at Fleming Park between Blue Springs and Lee's Summit. A collection of old structures, moved from seven western Missouri counties, depicting a typical 1850s farming community.

Museums at 18th and Vine. The Negro Leagues Baseball Museum and the American Jazz Museum are both housed in this historical area, 18th and Vine streets, Kansas City, Mo.

National Frontier Trails Center. 318 W. Pacific Ave., Independence, Mo. Museum and research center dealing with the settlement and exploration of the West, with a special focus on the Santa Fe, California and Oregon trails from the 1820s to the 1880s.

Shawnee Indian Mission Museum State Historical Site. 3403 W. 53rd St., Fairway, Kan. In buildings constructed from the 1830s on by the Rev. Samuel Johnson.

Treasures of the Steamboat Arabia. 400 Grand Blvd., Kansas City, Mo. Tells the story of a pre-Civil War Missouri River steamboat that sank just upstream from Kansas City.

Harry S. Truman Library and Museum. U.S. 24 and Delaware St., Independence, Mo. Contains a variety of exhibits and research materials concerning President Truman and his era.

Bruce R. Watkins Cultural Heritage Center. 3700 Blue Parkway, Kansas City, Mo. Commemorates the black community in the Kansas City metropolitan area through exhibits, films, lecture demonstrations, story telling, plays and other cultural activities.

ACKNOWLEDGMENTS

We would like to thank everyone who contributed information and suggestions to this volume, and particularly to those archivists and librarians who provided advice and help far beyond the call of duty.

David Boutros of the Western Historical Manuscript Collection-Kansas City provided a world of help and guidance from start to finish. He and his staff also turned up fascinating photographs and other images of life long ago.

Much information and many illustrations about Kansas City's past can be found at the Special Collections Department of the Kansas City Public Library. Stuart Hinds provided wonderful tips and worked hard to provide many of the beautiful photos in this volume.

Four people skilled in dealing with elementary pupils contributed immensely to this book. These teachers reviewed all its pages, pointing out where sentences were too jumbled and phrases too difficult. They are Dana Rachelle Bart, Cassandra Lopez, Jennifer Roe and Penny Selle

This book was distilled from *Kansas City: An American Story*, published by Kansas City Star Books in 1999. The authors of that volume deserve most of the credit for most of the information provided in this book. They are Rick Montgomery and Shirl Kasper.

Monroe Dodd
Daniel Serda

INDEX

About the authors

Monroe Dodd has occupied a variety of editing jobs at *The Kansas City Star* and *The Kansas City Times*. He holds a bachelor's degree in journalism and a master's degree in history from the University of Kansas. He lives in Shawnee, Kan.

Daniel Serda, a native of Kansas City, Kan., holds a master's degree in city planning from the Massachusetts Institute of Technology, and is a candidate for a Ph.D. in city design and development. He received an undergraduate degree in political science from Harvard University and served two years as a research associate in the department of history at the University of Missouri-Kansas City. He lives on Boston's north shore.

Photography and illustration

Images not credited here are from the files of *The Kansas City Star*.

These sources have been abbreviated:

SC/KCPL: Special Collections Department, formerly the Missouri Valley Room, Kansas City Public Library.

WHMC: Western Historical Manuscript Collection, University of Missouri-Kansas City.

i. SC/KCPL.

ii-iii. SC/KCPL.

iv-v. SC/KCPL.

vi. SC/KCPL.

vii. Fambrough Collection, WHMC.

3. Left: Buffalo Bill Historical Center, Cody, WY. Gift of the Coe Foundation. Top right: Courtesy Richard B. Scudder.

5. Osage: State Historical Society of Missouri, Columbia. Kansa: Kansas State Historical Society. Map: Map and Geography Library, University of Illinois-Champaign.

6. Lewis and Clark map: Library of Congress. Fort Osage map: SC/KCPL.

7. Maps: SC/KCPL. Chouteaus: Missouri Historical Society, St. Louis, MHS Collections.

8. Top left: Historical Photograph Collections, Washington State University Libraries. Top right: ASJCF, St Jerome 1602 - Livre I - 30 (Jesuit Archives, Saint-Jerome, Quebec, Canada). Bottom left: State Historical Society of Missouri, Columbia.

9. Shawnee, Delaware: State Historical Society of Missouri, Columbia.

10. Dave Eames, *The Star*.

11. Top: Joslyn Art Museum, Omaha, Nebraska. Gift of Enron Art Foundation. Boats: Dave Eames, The Star.

12. Arrival of the Caravan at Santa Fe: General Research Division, The New York Public Library, Astor, Lenox and Tilden Foundations. Barrels: National Frontier Trails Center, Independence, Mo. Illustrations: Dave Eames, *The Star*.

13. McCoy: Kansas State Historical Society. Jug: National Frontier Trails Center, Independence, Mo.

14. Top: Jackson County Records Center. Bottom: SC/KCPL.

16. Kansas State Historical Society.

17. Brown: Kansas State Historical Society. Union flag courtesy Jim Beckner, Lee's Summit. Anderson: State Historical Society of Missouri, Columbia. Confederate flag courtesy Jerry Vest, Kansas City, Kan.

18. Top map: Kansas State Historical Society. Contemporary map: Dave Eames, *The Star*.

19. Top lithograph: Missouri Historical Society, St. Louis. Handbook: SC/KCPL.

20. Top: SC/KCPL. Middle: State Historical Society of Missouri, Columbia.

21. Top and bottom left: Kansas State Historical Society. Right: SC/KCPL.

22. Bottom: Bingham, George Caleb - Order No. 11, oil on linen, State Historical Society of Missouri - Columbia.

23. Left: Strauss Portrait. Courtesy of the State Historical Society of Missouri-Columbia.

24. Wilborn & Associates.

27. Left: WHMC. Right: SC/KCPL.

28. Top left: WHMC.

29. Divers: WHMC. Graphic: Dave Eames, *The Star*.

30. SC/KCPL.

31. Cowboy: Wallace Kansas Collection, Kansas Collection, University of Kansas Libraries. Stockyards: WHMC. Painting courtesy American Hereford Association. Cans: Kansas State Historical Society. Canners: WHMC.

32. Top: SC/KCPL. Bottom left and bottom right: Kansas State Historical Society.

33. SC/KCPL.

34. Top: Kansas State Historical Society. Proclamation: State Historical Society of Missouri, Columbia.

35. All except bottom right: WHMC.

36. Top: WHMC. Bottom left and right: SC/KCPL.

37. All except bottom left: SC/KCPL.

38. Bottom: WHMC.

39. Top left, top right and bottom right: SC/KCPL.

40. Bottom right: SC/KCPL.

42. WHMC.

43. WHMC.

44. Top: Kansas State Historical Society. Bottom center: Wyandotte County Historical Society and Museum.

45. Map: SC/KCPL. Top right: WHMC. Bottom right: SC/KCPL. Bottom left, before and after: Kansas City, Missouri, Board of Parks and Recreation Commissioners.

46. Top and middle: SC/KCPL. Bottom left: WHMC. Bottom right: Kansas City Museum.

47. Top and new city hall: SC/KCPL. Left: WHMC.

48. Badge: WHMC.

49. Bottom left: Wyandotte County Historical Society and Museum.

50. Top left: SC/KCPL. Top center: Wyandotte County Historical Society and Museum.

52. Top: Kansas State Historical Society. Bottom right: WHMC. Bottom left: SC/KCPL.

53-54: All photos: WHMC.

55: Paseo: SC/KCPL.

56. SC/KCPL.

58. Top left: Kansas City Museum Association, Kansas City, MO. Right and bottom left: Liberty Memorial Museum and Archives.

59. SC/KCPL.

60. Top left: National Archives and Records Administration, Central Plains Region. Top right: SC/KCPL.

61: Left and top right: SC/KCPL. Girl running: WHMC. Schools: Kansas Collection, Kansas City, Kansas Public Library.

62: Top: Johnson County Museum. Bottom left: SC/KCPL.

63. Walt Disney film courtesy Doug Moore.

64. Monarchs: Courtesy Wilbur S. Rogan. Blues Pennant: Chappell's Restaurant & Sports Museum. Bottom right: Jackson County Historical Society.

67. Top: Jack Wally Collection, WHMC. Bottom left: SC/KCPL.

68. City Union Mission.

69. Top right: SC/KCPL.

72. SC/KCPL.

75. Left: Wyandotte County Historical Society and Museum. Center: Courtesy Mark Birnbaum.

76. Center: Wyandotte County Historical Society and Museum.

77. Left: Wyandotte County Historical Society and Museum. Bottom: Wilborn & Associates.

78. Top, bottom and center right: Wyandotte County Historical Society and Museum. Center left: Wilborn & Associates. Bottom right: SC/KCPL.

83. Top: SC/KCPL.

84. Bottom left: The Kansas City Spirit, 1951, by Norman Rockwell with John Atherton Courtesy the Hallmark Fine Art Collection, Hallmark Cards Inc. Kansas City, Missouri.

86. Top left and right: SC/KCPL.

87. Left: SC/KCPL.

92. Bottom left: SC/KCPL.

93. Bottom: Photo by Jim Overbay.

94. Left: Courtesy Kansas City Area Development Council.

96. Bottom left and right: Warner Collection, courtesy of the Kansas City Museum Association, Kansas City, MO.

101. Center right: Black Archives of Mid-America.

107. Tom Taylor.

113. "Missouri River Number 7" by John English, courtesy John English.

114. National Aeronautics and Space Administration.